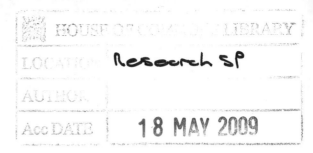

Disunited Kingdom

Disunited Kingdom

How the Government's
Community Cohesion Agenda
Undermines British Identity and Nationhood

David Conway

Civitas: Institute for the Study of Civil Society
London

First Published April 2009

© Civitas 2009
77 Great Peter Street
London SW1P 2EZ

Civitas is a registered charity (no. 1085494)
and a company limited by guarantee, registered in
England and Wales (no. 04023541)

email: books@civitas.org.uk

ISBN 978-1-906837-05-1

Typeset by
Civitas

Printed through
SS Media Ltd

Contents

Author

David Conway is a Senior Research Fellow at Civitas. His publications include *A Farewell to Marx; Classical Liberalism: The Unvanquished Ideal; Free-Market Feminism; The Rediscovery of Wisdom; In Defence of the Realm: The Place of Nations in Classical Liberalism* and *A Nation of Immigrants? A Brief Demographic History of Britain*. Before joining Civitas, Conway was Professor of Philosophy at Middlesex University and Head of its School of Philosophy and Religious Studies.

Acknowledgement

I should like to thank Nicholas Cowen for his astute editorial help with an earlier version of the manuscript.

Foreword

This examination by David Conway of the arguments both for and against faith schools represents the second study of the issue to be published by Civitas within the space of a few months. It follows Denis MacEoin's companion volume *Music, Chess and Other Sins*, published online in February 2009.[1]

The last time Civitas published on this topic was in 2001 when, again within the space of a few months, two titles appeared. Norman Dennis's book *The Uncertain Trumpet*,[2] published in August, looked at the involvement of the church in education in Britain and showed that, from the days of the Celtic monks until well into the nineteenth century, all formal education in Britain was religious education. The assumption of responsibility for education by the state only began in 1870, and Norman Dennis traced the decline of the religious influence on education from then until the present day. He argued that state funding and political control had combined to make church leaders so unsure of their position in education as to dilute religious education to the point at which it had ceased to have much influence. Instead of resisting the increasing secularisation of the culture, with its attendant moral relativism, church schools had largely colluded with it in what Norman Dennis described as a process resembling assisted suicide. Morality became 'the new "love that dare not speak its name"'.[3]

The second title, *Faith in Education*,[4] was published in September 2001 and consisted of essays by five authors on the strengths and weaknesses of faith schools, and the challenges they faced. Both of these titles had been inspired by the publication, at the end of 2000, of what was known as the Dearing Report. The Archbishops' Council of the Church of England had asked Sir Ron Dearing to chair a committee that would 'review the achievement of Church of England schools and... make proposals for their future development'.[5] The report was based on three key assumptions:

- that the demand for places in church schools far exceeded existing provision

- that is some important cities such as Newcastle, Norwich, Plymouth, Sunderland and Sheffield there were no maintained Church of England secondary schools

- that church schools were at the heart of the Church of England's mission to the nation

The Dearing Report recommended, amongst other things, the creation of another one hundred Church of England secondary schools to meet this under-provision, and the omens were initially favourable. In February 2001 the government published a green paper[6] welcoming the report's conclusions, which also received support from the other main political parties.

However, in the time it took to commission and bring to publication our two studies of the role of faith in education, an event of the greatest significance changed the whole framework of the debate. On 11 September 2001 the twin towers of the World Trade Centre in New York were demolished by planes flown by Islamist terrorists in the worst terrorist atrocity the world had ever seen. This provoked the most profound debate about the role of faith in a free society, particularly those versions of religious faith that hold in contempt the fundamental principles on which the free society is predicated. What price freedom of speech, freedom of worship and freedom of association, when they are being used by those who want to terminate these very freedoms? Should such people be given the liberty to spread their opinions?

Inevitably, these very serious concerns affected the discussion of faith schools, and the most immediately noticeable effect was the change in vocabulary—because we had previously spoken of church schools. All of the authors who contributed to our two 2001 books on the subject referred to church schools or denominational schools, i.e. schools under the control of the Church of England or the Roman Catholic church. There were a small number Jewish schools within the maintained sector, but no Muslim schools. The expansion of the Muslim population that had resulted from large-scale immigration had given rise to a growing number of private Muslim schools, and Muslim leaders had been arguing for some years that these should also qualify for support from public funds in the same way as Catholic, Anglican and Jewish schools.

Many people were inclined to agree, just on grounds of fairness, but 9/11 raised concerns that stalled that particular debate. Not wanting to appear especially prejudiced against any particular ethnic minority, people began to speak of faith schools when they really meant Muslim schools, and the debate is now couched entirely in terms of faith schools, with the term church schools having fallen out of use.

This is problematic. No one is really concerned that their local C of E primary is threatening social cohesion and fomenting acts of international terrorism, and it makes no sense to pretend otherwise. People may have these concerns about some Muslim schools, in which case it would help to be explicit about them, in order to discuss the evidence for and against such a proposition. The debate around an issue that concerns the very future of the free society is not helped by obfuscation. The argument that schools run by fundamentalist Christian and Jewish sects should be of as much concern as Islamist schools is a simplistic and dangerous diversionary tactic. When such Christian and Jewish fundamentalists start planting bombs on public transport, it will be time to subject the curricula in their schools to similar scrutiny.

Both Denis MacEoin and David Conway have concerned themselves mainly, in these books on faith schools, with the management of Muslim schools, whereas Muslim schools were not referred to at all in the two 2001 books. To such an extent has the debate changed. But both MacEoin and Conway make it clear that their target is not Muslims, but Islamists: those whose extreme and fundamentalist views threaten the very fabric of a free society. The majority of Muslims, like the majority of members of all faiths, want nothing more than to live in peace with their neighbours.

Robert Whelan

Summary

PART ONE: FAITH SCHOOLS AND COMMUNITY COHESION

1. Introduction: The Case Against Faith Schools   3-7

In January 2005, the chief inspector of schools David Bell drew opprobrium from many Muslim educationalists in Britain by accusing some of its independent Muslim schools of being social divisive in what they taught.

Many others had long expressed similar reservations about all faith schools, considering the segregating of children according to creed to be divisive.

Others accused faith schools of compromising the autonomy of their pupils in seeking to nurture faith in them. Others claim such schools allow middle-class parents to gain an unfair advantage for their children by enabling them to be bunched together at such schools through professing a faith, often not genuine.

2. Are Faith Schools Divisive?   8-11

Faced with the prospect of a steep increase in the number of Muslim schools seeking state funding, after the London suicide bombings of July 2005 those who feared their potential divisiveness called upon the state to cease funding new faith schools or else insist they reserve places for children of other faiths.

Many British Muslims want faith schools for their children and are aware how few of them the state supports relative to their numbers and the degree of support it gives to other faith groups. They deny that such schools are divisive.

3. Muslim Schools and Social Cohesion   12-23

Islam is no more inherently illiberal than other major religions. Attendance at moderate Muslim schools may immunise British-born Muslims against divisive forms of their religion more effectively than other forms of schooling.

Some independent Muslim schools, notably those linked with Deobandism, give rise to legitimate concern in terms of their potential divisiveness.

So does Ofsted's apparent inability or unwillingness to regulate them properly.

The provenance of the new Bridge Schools inspectorate for Muslim schools offers little reassurance it will regulate them more effectively in future.

4. Faith Schools in General and Social Cohesion   24-33

That all faith schools are inherently socially divisive is open to question.

It is unfair for the state only to fund schools other than faith schools when parents want the latter and they and faith groups are willing to meet their extra costs.

It is even more unfair for faith schools not to receive state funding, given that all state schools are legally required to provide a committed religious education.

The nurturance of religious faith by schools need be neither anti-educational nor oppressive, provided parents can withdraw their children from religious education and assemblies they find unconscionable. To deny such schools to children whose parents want them and are willing to meet the extra costs is unjust.

The overwhelming majority of the population of Britain is religiously affiliated, and so can be presumed to favour a religious education for children.

5. Faith Schools as Agents of Cohesion   34-45

In a society as diverse as Britain now is, there are several reasons why faith schools might be better able to promote cohesion than community schools. One reason is that they are better able than community schools to protect pupils belonging to vulnerable minorities from being bullied, currently a major problem in community schools.

A second reason why faith schools might be better able than community schools to promote cohesion is that they are able to elicit a better performance from their pupils, thereby rendering them more employable and so less likely to drift into crime.

There is no evidence that faith schools invariably disable or disincline pupils from mixing with those of other faiths. Indeed, there is contrary evidence.

6. Faith Schools and Pupil Autonomy 46-53

That faith schools seek to nurture faith need not be inherently prejudicial to the autonomy of their pupils. The outlook of young children is always non-autonomously formed. Faith schools can teach their pupils to be as open-minded as other schools.

Not to provide faith schools to young children from religious homes can be educationally damaging to them by sowing in them the seeds of confusion.

Religious schools are just as able, in principle, to cultivate open-mindedness and a spirit of critical enquiry in their pupils as other schools.

7. Faith Schools and Fairness 54-59

It is open to dispute that faith schools only achieve their generally better examination results by covert selection of more educable middle-class pupils.

Even if faith schools were to discontinue their selective admissions policies, it does not guarantee that children from different backgrounds would mix more.

8. Interim Conclusion 60-61

Faith schools have been found not to be inherently divisive. Some independent ones do give cause for concern, as does the failure of Ofsted to ensure their adequate inspection.

PART TWO: COUNTRY, CLASSROOMS AND COHESION

9. The Government's Community Cohesion Agenda
   — the Making of a Legend 65-73

Since the 2001 riots in Bradford, Burnley and Oldham, the Government has claimed that community cohesion is best promoted by different groups being made to mix and learn more about each other.

There is no truth in the claim that the 2001 riots resulted from increased self-segregation on the part of these towns' different groups, since there was no increased self-segregation on their part in the years before the riots. The districts where riots occurred had become more densely populated by South Asian Muslims, but for other reasons.

Official reports ignored evidence of mounting militancy for years among sections of the Muslim population of these towns, or else falsely attributed it to white racist provocation.

10. The Contact Hypothesis Examined   74-85

The claim that the 2001 riots resulted from lack of interaction between groups was based less on evidence than a theory known as the 'contact hypothesis'. This attributes poor inter-groups relations to prejudices and negative stereotypes born of lack of mutual knowledge and dealings.

There is no empirical evidence that a lack of close contact between groups inexorably makes for poor relations between them, as opposed to distant ones.

Nor is there any evidence that government-engineered contact between groups beyond what would spontaneously arise improves their mutual relations.

Even according to the Government's own measure of community cohesion, most parts of Britain enjoys high levels of it despite many of them being populated by diverse groups between whom there is little contact. The only exceptions arise in special circumstances: namely, when large influxes of foreign immigrants put pressure on local jobs and public services, and where large concentrations of South Asian Muslims are resident alongside whites.

11. School Twinning   86-90

Despite lacking evidence that it would improve inter-groups relations, the Government has encouraged the twinning of schools whose pupils come from different backgrounds.

Empirical studies of the effects of school twinning on the inter-group attitudes of pupils suggest such effects as it has are only adverse.

12. Forced Contact Between Communities   91-95

State-engineered contact between different groups that lack a common culture invariably causes conflict, since it threatens the defection of their members.

The results of a survey of over 30,000 Americans published in 2007 revealed diversity to have a depressive effect upon social capital, wherever it occurs.

13. Interculturalism—Meet the New Boss   96-109

A theory known as 'Interculturalism' lies behind the Government's efforts to make different groups mix and learn about each other.

The roots of interculturalism go back to war-time USA. But the original version of it emphasised the need for the culture of the majority to enjoy primacy and universal acceptance. Today's version is more multicultural in inflexion.

It is the revised multicultural version of interculturalism that drives the present Government's community cohesion agenda, especially in relation to schools.

The influence of interculturalism is especially conspicuous in the educational recommendations of Sir Keith Ajegbo's report on 'Identity and Diversity'.

14. A Closer Look at the Ajegbo Report   110-116

The Government has accepted several recommendations made by Ajegbo: notably, school-twinning; addition of a new strand on 'Identity and Diversity' to the citizenship curriculum; plus an annual 'Who do we think we are?' week.

School-twinning was considered earlier (Chapter 11) and found counter-productive.

The topics recommended for inclusion within the new Identity and Diversity strand, and their recommended coverage, seem calculated to undermine a sense of common belonging and national pride, especially among white pupils.

15. Interculturalism Refuted   117-119

The validity of the version of interculturalism currently in vogue is refuted by the success of a tried and tested way by which societies made diverse through foreign immigration have found cohesion:—viz. by immigrant assimilation.

16. A Better Pathway to Cohesion   120-126

To create social cohesion, assimilation does not require that immigrants or their descendants discard all native traditions of their countries of origin, provided these are compatible with the basic values of their new country.

The requisite form of assimilation, however, involves more than law-abidingness. It also demands immigrants accept the 'political culture' of their country of settlement and proficiency in its native language. Only then can a common sense of belonging and national identity be made to endure.

The Government's decision in 2007 to commission Lord Goldsmith to review citizenship suggests belated recognition of how its recent policies have eroded a sense of common belonging among native-born British citizens.

Lord Goldsmith's proposal that school-leavers should be able to pass through a citizenship ceremony seems unpromising, so long as most continue to leave school as ignorant of their country's history as they typically do today.

17. Conclusion: At the Going Down of the Sun   127-140

The main threats to community cohesion in Britain today emanate from excessive foreign immigration and the radicalisation of young British-born Muslims. These threats should be addressed, rather than the entire country forced to change in ways unlikely to do anything except exacerbate matters.

Faith schools generally do not threaten community cohesion in Britain, but some independent Muslim schools are divisive in terms of what they teach. They should be made to change or else close. Granting Muslim schools maintained status would be one way to ensure their moderation.

The best way schools can promote greater community cohesion is by being allowed to scrap most of what has recently been imposed on them in its name. Instead, they should be encouraged to teach Britain's history properly, giving much more attention to its Empire and the crucial, and often heroic, role colonials from all its parts played in its war efforts in the past.

Regional language policy needs revising to ensure that English remains the national language.

The only way Britain can remain cohesive is by its citizens acquiring a common sense of identity and belonging. This demands the privileging of its dominant native language and culture in its schools.

Ofsted is in need of urgent review if it is to remain up to the task of ensuring that schools are moderate in what they teach.

Ultimately, not just Britain's fate but that of the entire world depends on the victory of the liberal ideals it has championed in the course of its history.

Appendix: A Response to the Runnymede Trust Report   141-160

In December 2008, the Runnymede Trust published a report on the impact of faith schools upon community cohesion. It argued that their selective admissions policies and committed forms of religious education were socially divisive and in need of replacement by admissions policies and forms of pedagogy that did not privilege the faith of their sponsoring groups. The report also claimed that the committed forms of religious education provided by faith schools violated the right of their pupils to decide for themselves what to believe concerning religion, as well as which lifestyles and sexual orientation to adopt. The various considerations adduced by the Runnymede Report on behalf of its principal claims about faith schools are examined and found not to provide a compelling case. It is argued that the adoption by faith schools of the Report's principal recommendations would have a detrimental effect upon community cohesion, as well as an adverse effect upon the educational development of their pupils.

Upon the education of the people of this country the fate of this country depends.

Benjamin Disraeli

Part One

Faith Schools and Community Cohesion

1

Introduction:
The Case against Faith Schools

In January 2005, the then Chief Inspector of Schools David Bell delivered a talk to the Hansard Society on what it means to be a citizen.[1] His talk forms a useful starting-point for considering whether the state's current support of faith schools impedes or facilitates community cohesion in Britain today. Bell used the occasion of his talk to review how well the country's maintained secondary schools had gone about discharging their recently imposed statutory duty to teach citizenship as part of the National Curriculum. The report schools received from him was decidedly mixed. Some schools were said to have discharged their duty less conscientiously than others; some were said barely to have begun the task. It was, however, remarks that Bell made about certain independent faith schools that proved of greatest interest to the media, attracting as they did fierce hostility from some quarters of British society.

Bell began this controversial section of his speech innocuously enough, observing: 'Britain's diversity has the potential to be one of its greatest strengths. But diverse does not need to mean "completely different" and it certainly must not mean segregated or separate. Religious segregation in schools, for example, must not put our coherence at risk.'[2] He then drew attention to the recent proliferation of independent faith schools, notably Jewish, Muslim and Evangelical Christian ones. What finally set the cat among the pigeons, however, was when he expressed concern that: 'many young people are being educated in faith-based schools with little appreciation of their wider responsibilities and obligations to British society'.[3] To illustrate the source of his concern, Bell quoted a passage from a forthcoming annual Ofsted report on Muslim schools: 'Many schools must adapt their curriculum to ensure that it... helps [pupils to]... acquire an appreciation of and respect for other cultures in a way that promotes tolerance and harmony.' The clear implication of the passage that Bell quoted was that, in the opinion of Ofsted, Muslim schools were not doing enough to inculcate in their pupils the values of tolerance and harmony with non-Muslims.

Bell added: 'Many of these new schools are being opened by a younger generation of British Muslims who recognise that traditional Islamic education does not entirely fit pupils for their lives as Muslims in modern Britain.' Whether by accident or design, Bell's remarks left it unclear exactly what form of Islamic education this younger generation of British Muslims was offering. It is possible to interpret his remarks as having implied that the Muslim schools being opened were designed to provide a new alternative form of Islamic education better suited to life in Britain. But his remarks admitted of another interpretation. They could just as easily be construed as having implied that it was precisely because of their consciousness of how unsuited to life in modern Britain a traditional Islamic education was that this younger generation were opening Muslim schools to purvey it. On this understanding of what Bell had said, the implied purpose of these schools was to prevent their pupils from integrating into British society.

Whatever had been their precise intention, Bell's remarks had an immediate incendiary effect on several members of Britain's Muslim community with a special interest in education. Among those who took exception to them was Samira Eiturba, the head of a Muslim secondary school for girls in Huddersfield that had recently been placed joint third in the Kirklees secondary school league-tables. Responding to Bell, she said: 'Schools in this country have a lot of behavioural problems, but in Islamic schools the students learn responsibility and to be caring. Mr Bell should resign. Before he gives a lecture like this he should understand Islam.' [4]

No less incensed by Bell's remarks was Dr Muhammad Mukadam, chairman of the Association of Muslim Schools (AMSUK) an organisation mentioned by name by Bell. AMSUK is an umbrella group created in 1992 to support the development of full-time Muslim education in Britain that latterly had started to lobby for increased state support. Dr Mukadam is also head of a full-time Muslim school in Leicester that in 2001 had just been accorded voluntary-aided status. He was reported to have complained: 'I'm just as British as David Bell. What right has he got to say I'm constituting a threat? It was very hurtful. And what's the evidence? We should respect the right of people to be different, whether they're Christian, Hindu or whatever. A human being demands respect. He has to accept me for what I am. I'm a Muslim and I'm British. There's no contradiction.'[5]

Not all of Dr Mukadam's coreligionists have agreed with him that there was no contradiction between being Muslim and British. Events of the twenty-first century so far have served to persuade many in public life that faith schools are not the way forward to a harmonious integrated society in Britain. Barry Sheerman, chairman of the All Party House of Commons Select Committee on Education, voiced the feelings of many when he asked rhetorically: 'Do we want a ghettoised education system? Schools play a crucial part in integrating different communities and the growth of faith schools poses a real threat to this.'[6]

Of particular concern to the Labour MP was the decision of the Department for Education and Schools to award £100,000 to AMSUK to help it arrange the transfer into the maintained sector of some of its 60 or so affiliated independent schools. Barry Sheerman appeared not to be alone in having such concerns. An ICM poll commissioned by the *Guardian* newspaper in August of that same year found just under two-thirds of those polled agreed that 'the government should not be funding faith schools of any kind'.[7] Many had shared these concerns about faith schools long before the events of July 2005. Some of these concerns did not stem from any special worries about Muslim schools, but were directed at all faith schools. Some concerns, but not all, centred on their alleged social divisiveness. Faiths schools have been accused of perpetuating religious differences and encouraging religious sectarianism by causing children of different faiths to be educated, and have their religious beliefs reinforced, separately. This was one objection to faith schools and to state support for them levelled by ten British professional philosophers in a pamphlet published by the British Humanist Society in 2001 under the title *Religious Schools: the case against.*[8] They wrote:

> It is to be doubted whether separate schools for every religious persuasion are really the best way of promoting pluralism and tolerance in a multi-cultural society... If children grow up within a circumscribed culture, if their friends and peers are mostly from the same religion and hence also, very likely, the same ethnic group, and if they rarely meet or learn to live with others from different backgrounds, this is hardly calculated to promote the acceptance and recognition of diversity.[9]

However, that objection to faith schools was not what this group of humanist philosophers considered to be the most central. They contended that their chief failing was an educational fault from which they would suffer even if there were only one faith in society to which all adhered. In these circumstances, religion would not serve as a divisive force in society, but faith schools would still be vulnerable to their main objection: that faith schools have a debilitating effect on the intellectual and moral development of their pupils by nurturing a religious faith in them before they are of an age to decide for themselves whether to embrace it. Faith schools allegedly violate the autonomy, or rather potential autonomy, of their pupils by instilling in them beliefs and values that they acquire other than autonomously. The authors of the pamphlet wrote:

> The argument [against faiths schools] which we regard as the strongest... focuses on children's autonomy, or rather lack of it... Given the importance of fundamental religious and value commitments to a person's life, such commitments should be entered into only subject to all the normal requirements for valid consent: in particular, competence, full information, and voluntariness. Religious schools, however, are likely to violate these requirements—partly because of (younger) children's lack of autonomy and partly because of the nature of such schools' missions.[10]

In their pamphlet, the humanist philosophers drew attention to another feature of maintained faith schools that some have considered to be objectionable and a sufficient reason for the state not to support them, at least in their present form. Unlike other state schools, faith schools with voluntary-aided status are able to draw up and implement their own admission policies. When over-subscribed by applicants, in allocating places they are allowed to give priority to children whose parents adhere, or at least profess to adhere, to the faith that they seek to nurture. Many critics of these schools claim middle-class parents use such 'faith schools' to evade the non-selective admissions policies that many local education authorities have imposed on other state schools. They thereby are allegedly able to concentrate their more educable, because more privileged, children within these schools to the detriment of children from less favoured backgrounds who tend to end up in community schools. These latter children are thereby said to be unfairly penalised by faith schools because they are deprived of the benefits of being taught alongside more educable children. The humanist philosophers formulated this concern about faith schools as follows:

> While most Church schools are not officially permitted to select children on the basis of their class, behaviour or intelligence, there is little doubt that selection does take place... Precisely because they have a good reputation, religious schools are sought out by ambitious and resourceful parents, both believers and non-believers; and as these tend to be the sort of parents who produce ambitious and resourceful children, high standards are perpetuated... Many people who support the principles of comprehensive education are opposed to Church schools not, or not only, because of their confessional character, but because many of them operate as 'grammar schools by another name'.[11]

We have now identified three objections to faith schools and their support by the state: (1) faith schools are socially divisive and inimical to community cohesion, especially those Muslim schools that purvey a more traditional form of Islamic education; (2) faith schools impair the intellectual and moral development of their pupils by nurturing in them beliefs and values in a way that disinclines or disables them from reviewing them critically later; (3) faith schools help to perpetuate the unequal life-chances of children to the special detriment of those of them least advantaged by birth and background. Even though it might not be possible to prevent parents from privately educating their children in such schools, many have claimed that the state should not assist them in doing so. We shall now consider the merits of each objection.

2

Are Faith Schools Divisive?

After the London suicide-bombings of July 2005, renewed concerns were voiced about the potentially deleterious effect of faith schools on social cohesion. Their expression suggested an underlying concern that they all served to keep Muslim and non-Muslim children apart, thereby reinforcing their mutual segregation in ways that could be dangerous. Barry Sheerman has said of the Government's standing commitment to fund still more of them: 'These things need to be thought through very carefully before they are implemented.'

The Government had previously signalled its support for more voluntary-aided religious schools shortly after the July 2001 riots, but before the attack on the New York Trade Towers and the Pentagon on September 11th of that same year. These attacks renewed concern that, once created, state-funded Muslim schools would be difficult to close and yet might make it harder for the Muslim community to integrate into British society. The Government's dilemma arose from the fact that very few Muslim schools had been accorded voluntary-aided status in comparison with those of other faith communities. To withhold that status from the independent Muslim schools risked antagonising many in the Muslim community who could claim on that basis that they were being treated as second-class citizens. On the other hand, to accede to their requests would be to invite the proliferation of such schools in greater number than had already occurred, as more and more were created and then sought to gain the benefits of state-funding.

Faced with this dilemma, some voices were heard suggesting that the best way out of it would be for the state to cease to support any more faith schools. Then the number of independent Muslim schools would be less likely to grow, and the risk of the indefinite segregation of Muslims and non-Muslims would be reduced. If withdrawal of state funding from all faith-schools were politically impossible, then the next best way to defuse the problem they posed would be for the state to demand of those that sought funding that they should set aside quotas for children of other faiths or of none. The Government did indeed attempt to incorporate a clause imposing such a requirement into the

Education and Inspections Act of 2006. It was obliged to withdraw that clause in the face of concerted opposition from the Roman Catholic and Jewish communities. They claimed such quotas would damage the distinctive ethos of their faith schools as well as deny places to children who belonged to their faiths and for whom they had been established.

To understand the Government's dilemma, one needs to appreciate how few voluntary-aided schools Muslims in England have in comparison with other faith groups, and relative to the respective sizes of their school-age populations. Table 2.1 gives some indication.

Table 2.1
Number of Faith Schools in England and
Number of School-Age Children at Them

	Christian	Muslim	Sikh	Jewish	Hindu
Number of Children 4-15 Years	5,098,930	378,340	62,237	33,292	82,952
Number at Maintained Faith Schools	1,710,410	1,770	640	14,670	0
Number of Faith Schools:					
Maintained	6,802	7	2	37	0
Independent	700	115	0	38	0

N.B. The number of children aged 4-15 years is for 2001. The number of children at maintained schools is for 2005. The number of schools is for 2007. One Hindu school within the maintained sector opened in September 2008.

Source: *Faith in the System*, Department for Children, Schools and Families, 2007

The Muslim community and the British Government are aware of this gross anomaly. Just six per cent of Muslim schools receive state funding, as against over ninety per cent of Christian schools and just below fifty per cent of Jewish schools. Moreover, whereas a third of Christian children of school-age attend maintained Christian schools and nearly half of Jewish children of school-age attend maintained Jewish schools, fewer than five per cent of Muslim children attend maintained Muslim schools. By no means all Muslim parents want their children to attend a Muslim school, but many thousands more do than there are currently places at Muslim schools within the maintained sector. The demand for such schools is partly shown by the three-fold increase in the number of independent Muslim schools in the ten-year period between 1995 and 2005.[1] It is also indicated by the declared preferences of Muslim parents. An ICM poll of British Muslims conducted in 2004 found that nearly half of those polled wished their children to attend a Muslim school. [2]

In a White Paper published in September 2001 entitled *Schools: Achieving Success*, the Government had signalled its willingness to increase the number of faith schools within the maintained sector, where there was proven parental demand for them and local approval. Its stated reasons were to increase parental choice and because pupils at faith schools had been found to achieve better results in public examinations, which the Government attributed to their religious 'ethos'. The events of September 11th, and even more the July 2005 suicide-bombings, called into question the wisdom of their expansion. This was especially so in the case of Muslim schools.

On both occasions, educationalists from the Muslim community responded to these concerns by denying that Muslim schools were divisive. To the contrary, they claimed, such schools would be best able to exert a moderating influence upon young Muslims growing up in Britain. Rafaqat Hussain, president of a Birmingham-based Muslim educational charity created in 1985 that had successfully obtained state funding for several schools, was quoted as saying shortly after the September 11th terror attacks:

> This is not educational apartheid: this is allowing children to be educated in a familiar atmosphere where they can have prayers at the right time without the timetables clashing, and where other issues important to our faith can be accommodated. They will still be integrating into the community outside of school hours. Muslim parents are already in fear that we are losing our youth and that values are not being passed on. Events in Bradford were a wake-up call to many who saw young men rioting in such a shocking way. There is growing concern that we must go back to traditional values and those are not being met in inner-city comprehensives.[3]

Similarly, shortly after the London suicide-bombings in July 2005, Muhammad Mukadam, chairman of the Association of Muslim Schools, was quoted as claiming that:

[Muslim schools] turned out rounded citizens, more tolerant of others and less likely to succumb to criminality or extremism. We give our young people confidence in who they are and an understanding of Islam's teaching of tolerance and respect which prepares them for a positive and fulfilling role in society. Often Muslim children in mixed secondary schools feel isolated and confused about who they are. This can cause disaffection and lead them into criminality, and the lack of a true understanding of Islam can ultimately make them more susceptible to the teachings of fundamentalists.[4]

Dr Mukadam rightly pointed out that none of the British Muslims convicted following the riots in Bradford and Oldham in 2001 or any of those linked to the London bombings had been to Islamic secondary schools. That remains a highly pertinent fact. But is it enough to absolve Muslim schools in particular and other faith schools more generally from the charge that they are socially divisive and inimical to community cohesion? This question will be dealt with in two stages, first, considering solely Muslim schools, and then faith schools more generally.

11

3

Muslim Schools and Social Cohesion

Any suggestion that Muslim schools pose a greater threat, in principle, to community cohesion in Britain than do other varieties of faith school must be fiercely resisted. While some apostate Muslims have claimed that Islam is inherently incompatible with western liberal democracy, there is no reason to take their word on this subject, rather than that of Muslim scholars, like Mohamed Charfi, who have argued to the contrary.[1] Islam is no less amenable than other revealed religions to different interpretations. Of the different varieties of Islam possible because of the inherent indeterminacy it shares in common with all other world religions, some versions of Islam are every bit as compatible with liberal democratic values and institutions as are the countless many different varieties of Judaism and Christianity that have equally managed to achieve accommodation and become compatible with the values and institutions of liberal modernity.

Furthermore, as Rafaqat Hussain and Muhammad Mukadam have both suggested, attendance at a Muslim school in which one of these many moderate versions of Islam were nurtured could well be likely to provide many young British Muslims growing up in Britain today with an understanding of that faith that would be likely to immunise them more effectively against the siren calls of extremists. They would be less likely to be persuaded that their religion called for or licensed acts of violent extremism against their non-Muslim compatriots. This point is made by Paul Goodman, Shadow Minister for Community Cohesion. In a talk to the New Culture Forum in January 2008 entitled 'Not Enough Islam? How mainstream Islam can challenge extremism', Goodman observed that: 'While there are no easy or guaranteed means of ensuring this, I've come to believe that if young Muslim men know more about their own religion they are less likely to be drawn on to the conveyor belt to terrorism. In other words, one of the problems we face isn't that there is too much mainstream Islam among Britain's Muslim communities, but too little.'[2]

This having been said, there is nevertheless still cause for concern about several independent Muslims schools in Britain whose heads have been known to espouse or otherwise support immoderate forms of Islam, as does their affiliated madrassa in India. This is the group of so-called Deobandi madrassas. They are mostly residential boys' schools, largely situated in the north of England. Many are affiliated to the Dar Ul-Uloom (literally: 'House of God') in Deoband India, the world-wide headquarters of the Deobandi movement. It was established ten years after the Indian Mutiny of 1857 to provide young Muslims with a form of Islamic education that would immunise them against British culture. The tone of animosity towards all things British that inspired its founding is reflected in the assertion of one of its founders who said: 'The English have perpetrated boundless acts of tyranny against the Muslims for their... uprising of 1857... They have left no stone unturned to plunder and obliterate the Islamic arts and science, Muslim culture and civilisation.'[3] The curriculum developed and employed at this Deoband madrassa was designed to prevent students from acquiring any elements of British culture: 'English was prohibited... and all students began their studies by learning the Qur'an by heart in the original Arabic. All classes thereafter were focused on Quranic studies... [T]he school promoted an uncompromising, puritanical and exclusive fundamentalism... [and] retained militant jihad as a central pillar of faith... Students as young as five were accepted and often remained there until adulthood.'[4] By 1976, this Deobandi madrassa had established nearly 9,000 schools world-wide.[5] By 2001, their number had increased to over 15,000, of which several had been established in Britain.[6]

The first Deobandi madrassa to be created in Britain was established by an alumnus of several Deobandi madrassas in India who immigrated to Britain in 1968. This was Yusuf Motala. In 1975, he opened a boys' residential madrassa in Bury of which he remains head.[7] Reportedly, the school was opened with financial help from the Saudi Arabian embassy.[8] Its alumni have since established 26 other Deobandi madrassas in Britain. It has been estimated they have produced as many as 80 per cent of Britain's home-grown Muslim clerics.[9] Among these alumni is Riyadh ul Haq, an immigrant to Britain from Gujarat. After leaving the Bury madrassa, he went on to establish and head two such madrassas, one in Kidderminster, the other in Leicester.

Ul-Haq's numerous sermons suggest that his schools might not be best suited towards promoting community cohesion. He has claimed that non-Muslims hate Muslims and Islam,[10] has extolled violent jihad,[11] and has called upon British Muslims not to befriend non-Muslims.[12] He has also asserted that: 'The Jews and Christians will never be content with you or pleased with you until you follow their way, i.e. completely, in everything.'[13] Another alumnus from the same Bury Deobandi madrassa is Dr Mahmood Chandia. In one of his sermons, he claimed that music was a way in which Jews spread a 'Satanic web' with which to ensnare and corrupt young Muslims. He also claimed that: 'Nearly every university in England has a department which is called the music department, and in others, where the Satanic influence is more, they call it the Royal College of Music.'[14] Dr Chandia lectures in Islamic Studies at Manchester Metropolitan University and is subject leader of Islamic Studies at the University of Central Lancashire.[15]

Other Deobandi-influenced madrassas in Britain affiliated with the Tablighi Jamaat movement, literally 'Party of Preachers', also pose a problem for community cohesion. Founded in India in the 1920s by another alumnus of the Dar Ul-Uloom madrassa in Deoband, Tablighi Jamaat is an ultra-pietistic, pan-national Muslim movement that also seeks to discourage Muslims from adopting Western ways or fraternising with non-Muslims, save to win them over to Islam. In 1995, one of their most fervent supporters who had settled in Britain in 1972 called upon his fellow Muslim parents there to: 'Save your progeny from the education of [state] school and college in the same way as you [would] save them from a lion or a wolf... To send them in the atmosphere of college is as dangerous as [to] throw them into hell with your own hands.'[16] The following year, he wrote: 'A major aim of *tabligh* is to rescue the *Ummah* from the culture and civilisation of the Jews, Christians and [other enemies] of Islam and to create such hatred for their ways as humans have for urine and excreta.'[17]

The European headquarters of the Tablighi Jamaat movement are situated at the Markazai Masjid ('Central Mosque') in Dewsbury, West Yorkshire. With a capacity to hold 5,000, this mosque opened in 1982, after having reportedly been built with funding from Saudi Arabia.[18] Members of Tablighi Jamaat vociferously oppose violent extremism, but many known violent extremists have had links with the movement or have attended its activities. These include the 'American Taleban' John Walker Lindh, 'shoe bomber' Richard Reid, and Mohammed Siddiqui Khan and Shehzad Tanweed, two of the July 2005 London tube-train suicide bombers. They also include several British-born young Muslim men found guilty of terror-related offences over the alleged conspiracy that was uncovered in 2006 to plant bombs on transatlantic aeroplanes and detonate them while in flight.[19]

Despite eschewing acts of violent extremism, Tablighi Jamaat has nonetheless been described as a 'gateway to terrorism', on the grounds that its separatist ideology provides an environment conducive to jihadist recruitment. Khaled Abou El Fadl, professor of Islamic Law at UCLA, explains:

> You teach people to exclude themselves, that they don't fit in, that the modern world is an aberration, and offence, some form of blasphemy… By preparing them in this fashion, you are preparing them to be in a state of warfare against this world… I don't believe there's a sinister plot where they're in bed with Osama bin Laden but are hiding it. But I think that militants exploit the alienated and withdrawn social attitude created by the Tablighis by fishing in the Tablighi pond.[20]

Attached to the Dewsbury mosque is a residential madrassa for boys aged between 12 and 16 years. Known as the Institute of Islamic Education (or Jaamia Talimul Islam), it is intended to serve as a seminary for the training of imams and teachers of Islam and many of its hundred or so pupils stay there for several years after turning 16 to complete their studies. When inspected by Ofsted in early 2005, the curriculum of the school was judged to 'lack breadth' and to devote not enough time to secular subjects.[21] While teaching of Islamic subjects was judged 'never less than satisfactory and often good', a considerable amount of teaching was judged 'unsatisfactory or poor'. Ofsted reported that: 'the weaker lessons are characterised by inadequate planning, unsatisfactory classroom organisations and the poor assessment of pupils' abilities. Pupils' books are rarely marked.'

The school does not allow pupils to read newspapers or listen to radio or television programmes. Nor does it take its pupils on any organised visits, other than to go out preaching, since it believes such visits would 'distract pupils from their studies'. Despite all this, Ofsted judged the school to have met the requirements for registration in

15

respect of its statutory duty to promote the 'spiritual, moral, social and cultural development of pupils'.

Following a second inspection of the school in May 2008, Ofsted reported that its 'secular curriculum... has improved since the previous inspection'. It delivered this judgement despite finding some of the short-term lesson planning in secular subjects at the school still 'unsatisfactory'.[22] Ofsted reported that pupils had 'few opportunities... to experience out of school activities as part of their social and cultural development', and that the school needed to develop how it made pupils 'aware about British public institutions'. Despite all these reservations, Ofsted judged it provided 'a good quality of education for its students' and promoted 'tolerance and respect for other faiths'.

At the time of the first Ofsted inspection, the school's joint head was Dr Mohammed Mulk. He is the father of Ms Aisha Azmi, the classroom assistant who, in March 2007, lost her appeal against dismissal from a Church of England primary school in Dewsbury for refusing to remove her niqab when teaching English to pupils learning it as a second language. To concerns raised by Ofsted about his overly narrow focus on Islamic subjects, Dr Mulk responded by telling a *Times Educational Supplement* reporter: 'Parents send their children here for an Islamic education. They don't want their sons to take exams.'[23]

Since the Tablighi mosque opened in Dewsbury in 1992, the Saville Town area in which it is situated has seen its Indian population grow by 25 per cent, and its Pakistani population grow by 60 per cent. Its 5,000 strong population is now 88 per cent Asian. As a result, it has been observed that: 'it is possible for a Muslim child to grow up [there]—in the family home, at school and in the mosque and madrassa —without coming into contact with Western lifestyles, opinions or values'.[24]

One is entitled to wonder how happy all Muslim parents must be with the curriculum of this Dewsbury madrassa, despite it being heavily oversubscribed with six applicants for every place. A former alumnus of it has stated that 'the profile of his classmates [was]... from poor, uneducated backgrounds... [and] that some families chose the seminary as a way of ensuring their offspring were simply housed and fed for 11 months of the year.'[25] Certainly, with residential fees at only £1,410 per annum in 2008, it seemingly provides an extremely cheap subsistence for a child from a hard-pressed family.

In its 2005 report Ofsted claimed that, because 'pupils are encouraged to volunteer for service, within the Institute, such as serving at meals, and in the wider community, for example, through travelling in groups to mosques and homes inviting Muslims to increase their practice of Islam, ... [t]he madrassah curriculum is therefore vocational training for the role of social worker within the Muslim community'. Describing serving food and calling on co-religionists to become more observant as social work training seems strained to the point of being misleading. The current statutory instrument which empowers Ofsted to inspect such schools in England is the Education (Independent School Standards) Regulations of 2003 no. 1910. According to these regulations, schools must satisfy Ofsted that they provide 'adequate preparation of pupils for the life opportunities, responsibilities and experiences of adult life' or else they are ineligible for registration [Regulation 2 (j)]. It is seriously open to question whether the narrow curriculum taught at the Dewsbury madrassah and at other similar schools adequately prepares pupils for adult life in Britain, even, or perhaps especially, as religious leaders and teachers.

Dr Dilwar Hussain, head of the Policy Research Unit of the Islamic Foundation, has observed of this kind of curriculum:

> Much of our current training seems to prepare people not to live in this world—but to leave this world! How often do we hear of Imams being taught the salient features of modern Western knowledge—grappling with the complexities of modernity, learning about European philosophy, art, culture and heritage?... [T]he spirit of contextualisation is, on the whole, missing from the education process. Unless we are able to equip Imams with the tools to work in British society, how can we expect them to confidently deal with the pastoral care of, say, young Muslims, or enter into inter-faith dialogue, build bridges within the neighbourhood or engage the local political community? My criticism is hence not directed at individual Imams but at the system for training and employing Imams... [26]

Ofsted has powers to judge that a school does not meet the conditions for registration when its curriculum does not adequately prepare their pupils for adult life in Britain. One condition is that the curriculum should 'give pupils experience in... human and social, physical and aesthetic and creative education', enable them 'to acquire skills in speaking and listening, [and] literacy... skills', and provide 'adequate preparation of pupils for the opportunities, responsibilities and experiences of adult life.' [Regulation 5.1(a), (c) and (j)] Another is that they should 'promote principles which... provide pupils with a broad general knowledge of public institutions and services in England... [and which] assist pupils to acquire an appreciation of... other cultures in a way that promotes tolerance and harmony between different cultural traditions'. [Regulation 5.2 (d) and (e)].

As has been seen in the case of the Institute of Islamic Education, Ofsted seems reluctant to demand Muslim schools satisfy certain conditions to qualify for registration, even when their inspection reveals inadequacies. In February 2008, Ofsted carried out an inspection of Jamia Al Hudaa, an independent Muslim secondary school for boys in Sheffield. Ofsted found the school did not meet all the registration conditions. Its failings related both to the curriculum which did 'not prepare pupils well enough for the experiences, responsibilities and challenges of adult life',[27] and to the spiritual, moral, social and cultural development of pupils that did not provide 'pupils with enough information about the public institutions and services of England'. Ofsted also found that pupils had only 'a very limited understanding of faiths and cultures different from their own', yet the school was not required by Ofsted to teach about those other faiths and cultures. It is hard to see why not, given that one of the conditions of their eligibility for registration is that independent faith schools promote principles that assist their pupils 'to acquire an appreciation... of other cultures... in a way that promotes tolerance and harmony'.

Another pair of independent residential Muslim schools that give different cause for concern in relation to community cohesion are the Jamia al-Karam and Al-Karam in Retford, Nottinghamshire. This concern relates to some of their extra-curricula activities. Both schools were founded by their current head, Muhammad Imdad Hussain Pirzada. Shortly after the start of the second Palestinian Intifada in January 2001, Pirzada visited the Palestinian occupied territories to distribute aid to widows, orphans and those injured in the fighting. A charity that he founded and runs from one of his schools had raised the aid distributed on his visit, during which he made the acquaintance of Yusuf Abu Sneina, imam of Jerusalem's Al-Aqsa mosque. Pirzada has since invited Abu Sneina to stay at his school and address its pupils. In March 2003, shortly after the American invasion of Iraq, Abu Sneina reportedly delivered a sermon at the Al Aqsa mosque, broadcast by the Palestinian Authority radio station Voice of Palestine, in which he said: 'Our enemies should be confronted by men having faith in God... TV reports [show]... ugly massacres by the US and British invasion forces. This is a disgrace. God, help our Muslim people in Iraq be victorious over the infidels. God destroy the enemies of the Muslims... God destroy them all.'[28] In September 2005, Abu Sneina said: 'Anyone who watches closely the nature of our world today can see that the heretical countries—first and foremost, the USA—have succeeded greatly in tearing our Islamic world apart... It is terrorism, and there's no choice but to fight it.'[29] Since delivering these two sermons, Abu Sneina has visited England on several occasions on the invitation of Pirzada, sharing the platform with him at events organised by alumni of his schools.[30] In June 2006, Abu Sneina stayed as Pirzada's guest at the Al-Karam school. According to an account on the school's website, Abu Sneina addressed its pupils on 'a range of issues [including]... the problems Muslims are facing in the world.'[31] Given his earlier sermons, one hopes that his opinions by then had changed as to what those problems were that Muslims were facing and how they should go about trying to solve them.

Several other independent Muslim schools have been found to purvey versions of Islam singularly ill-suited towards promoting community cohesion in Britain. The most notorious of them is the Saudi-funded King Fahad Academy in West London. In April 2008, a former teacher at the school was found to have been unfairly dismissed from it and awarded substantial damages by an employment tribunal. The school had dismissed him for having complained to Edexcel that staff there in 2006 had allowed pupils to bring into their GCSE examinations heavily annotated course books. When he had suggested to the school that it might be seeking to cover up his allegation, the tribunal was told that a senior colleague had remarked to him: 'This is not England. It is Saudi Arabia.'[32] Among pupils at the fee-paying school were children of Abu Hamza and Abu Qatada. A query by the teacher concerning their ability to pay the fees while they were being said to be claiming benefits drew the response that he should mind his own business.[33] The most worrying aspects about the school to which the teacher drew attention were the contents of some of its textbooks. One such book used to teach children as young as five described Jews as apes and Christians as pigs and invited them to mention repugnant characteristics of Jews.[34] Other textbooks called upon Muslims 'to avoid any sort of engagement with non-believers, such as attending their celebrations, showing happiness "on their festivals", offering them sympathy or condolences, or cooperating in artistic activities like singing, dancing, theatre, and taking part in sports'.[35] Another Saudi textbook found at the school portrayed the *Protocols of the Elders of Zion* as an authentic Jewish text in which was outlined a real secret Jewish conspiracy to dominate the world through a variety of nefarious means.[36] Yet another Saudi textbook found at the school stated that: 'Jews are a people who were moulded with treachery and backstabbing throughout the centuries and they do not keep their word nor honour their promise.'[37]

What makes this case of such concern is that, in March 2006, the school had undergone inspection by Ofsted and had been found 'to provide very well for its pupils' spiritual development'.[38] That Ofsted could have so badly misjudged the quality of education provided at the King Fahad Academy offers little consolation for knowing how few independent Muslim schools Ofsted has chosen to inspect regularly. According to a newspaper report in March 2007: 'More than half of private Muslim schools have not been inspected for five years, while some have not received a full inspection for a decade.'[39] The apparent failure by Ofsted to inspect independent Muslim schools as thoroughly and regularly as it should have is of especial concern, given how poorly it has judged those it has inspected with regard to teaching tolerance. Of 50 Muslim schools that were inspected by Ofsted in 2004, 18 were cited by it as having failed to teach tolerance.[40]

Given their distinctive character, Ofsted might have considered itself ill-equipped to carry out inspections of independent Muslim schools. This might have been why, in January 2008, the Government announced a new independent inspectorate to examine these schools, over which Ofsted would merely keep a watching brief. To be known as the Bridge Schools Inspectorate (BSI), this new independent schools inspectorate is the joint creation of AMSUK and of the Christian Schools Trust (CST). The latter is an umbrella organisation for 50 evangelical schools which BSI will also inspect in addition to the 60 independent Muslim schools affiliated to AMSUK. The remaining Muslim schools will be inspected by Ofsted directly, or else possibly by another body, the Independent Schools Inspectorate (ISI), created in 1999 for the 50 per cent of independent schools that belong to the Independent Schools Council and that feared Ofsted did not understand their distinctive ethos. BSI was not created on the initiative of Ofsted but was the result of separate approaches by AMSUK and CST, each seeking an independent inspectorate better suited to the ethos of their schools.[41] When the new independent inspectorate was announced, AMSUK and CST issued a joint statement:

> Our aim is to ensure that our schools are the best that they can be so that our students can achieve well academically and become well-adjusted citizens. We desire our inspections to be rigorous, objective and transparent. We believe this inspectorate can be a model of how different faiths and cultures can come together to serve a common purpose and contribute to greater community cohesion.[42]

While this spirit of inter-faith cooperation is heartening to those concerned to strengthen community cohesion, not everyone has welcomed Ofsted's delegation of its responsibility to the BSI. Barry Sheerman, chairman of the House of Commons Select Committee on Education, described the development as being 'very worrying'. A month earlier he had informed MPs that some local councils were finding it 'difficult to know what is going on in some faith schools'.[43] Moreover, in September 2006, former Conservative Secretary of State for Education, Lord Baker, had already described the idea of AMSUK setting up its own inspectorate as 'outrageous and extraordinary' and a retrogressive step in terms of community cohesion:

> If there is a separate inspectorate for Muslim schools, it'll be much easier for extremists to infiltrate them and to radicalise students. It's the way towards a more divided society, an independent Muslim community in our country. If we're going to have a harmonious society where extremists are brought within the fold this is not the way forward.[44]

Dr Mukadam, who as was mentioned earlier is the chairman of AMSUK, responded to what Lord Baker had said by denying there was *any* evidence faith schools created division or segregation.[45] He might well be correct that there is no evidence that *all* faith schools do. However, the facts about some Muslim schools detailed above, plus the activities and statements also detailed of some of their heads, provide strong circumstantial evidence that *some* Muslim schools are likely to be divisive and to encourage segregation. The denial by the chairman of

21

AMSUK that there is any evidence that any Muslim schools are divisive hardly offers reassurance that the new Bridge Schools inspectorate that his organisation helped to create and of which he is a director will carry out their inspection with any greater diligence or proficiency than Ofsted.

There are several other reasons to wonder whether the new inspectorate for independent Muslim schools will be likely to do a better job than the poor job that Ofsted did to ensure that none are divisive in terms of what they teach. Immediate oversight of the new inspectorate is the shared task of AMSUK and of the Christian Schools Trust. The chairman of AMSUK and a director of the new inspectorate is Dr Mukadam who is also a principal of a Muslim secondary school in Leicester. In May 2002, Ofsted carried out an inspection of the school when it was still an independent one and still combined with a Muslim primary school from which Dr Mukadam's school has since become separated. Ofsted found several failings with the school. These included 'many... shortcomings... highlighted in the... inspection report of 1999... [that] have not yet been acted upon.'[46] One criticism that Ofsted levelled at that part of this school for which Dr Mukadam was then responsible was its failure to prepare pupils to take their place in the wider society after leaving it. The report stated:

> One of the school's declared aims is to encourage pupils 'to realise their full potential in order to take their place as responsible and contributing members of the wider society'. This aim could be strengthened to include pupils' understanding of citizenship and to prepare then to take their place in the wider society.[47]

This criticism was levelled at a school whose head at the time is now a director of the new inspectorate whose job it is to ensure that Muslim schools are not divisive.

The deputy chairman of AMSUK is Ibrahim Hewitt. He too is a head of an independent Muslim school situated in Leicester. Between 2004 and 2006, Hewitt was Assistant Secretary General of the Muslim Council of Britain. Some of Hewitt's pronouncements make one wonder just how able and determined to root out divisiveness from Muslim schools will be an inspectorate of them oversight of which partially falls to an organisation of which he is the deputy chair. In March 2004, Hewitt reportedly said that: 'Integration should not be mentioned in a democracy.'[48] In 2005, he also defended the then policy of the Muslim Council of Britain not to take part in Holocaust Memorial Day on the grounds that its commemoration was offensive to Muslims since it was overly focused on crimes against Jews. At the time, Hewitt defended the policy by stating: 'There are 500 Palestinian towns and villages that have been wiped out over the years. That's pretty genocidal to me.'[49] Since Hewitt is deputy chairman of the organisation that helped to create and now jointly oversees the new inspectorate for independent Muslim schools, one is entitled to wonder just how keen and able it will be to ensure that none are divisive.

Even if it could be ensured that no Muslim schools were any more divisive than any other variety of faith school, the general charges against all faith schools would remain: that they were unworthy objects of state-funding because of their inherent divisiveness. As a signatory to the United Nations' Universal Declaration of Human Rights, Britain could never deny parents the right to send a child to a religious school if they wanted to. Article 26 of the Declaration expressly acknowledges parents have the 'right to choose the kind of education that shall be given to their children'. It is, however, one thing for the state to tolerate religious schooling of a moderate kind, when parents want it for their children and they and their faith communities are prepared to pay for it themselves. It is quite another for the state to help to make religious schooling freely available to parents. Can state-funding of any faith schools be justified in a religiously and ethnically plural society concerned to promote community cohesion? That is the question to which we now turn.

4

Faith Schools in
General and Social Cohesion

As a result of the volume of immigration since the end of World War Two, Britain has become far more ethnically and religiously diverse than it has ever previously been. Undoubtedly, this presents a significant challenge for social cohesion. So long as Britain remains a nation state, or at least so long as England does should the United Kingdom break up in the near future, social cohesion requires that all citizens acquire a common sense of belonging to one and the same nation, with appropriate mutual identifications, attachments and loyalties. Must a plurality of faith schools necessarily impede the formation of a common sense of national identity in their pupils? Many of their critics *claim* they must. But evidence advanced for that claim is less than conclusive, and there is counter-balancing evidence that may be cited to support the opposite view.

It is true that faith schools segregate children along lines of faith and thereby often separate them along ethnic lines too. Such segregated schooling, however, does not by itself make the development of a sense of common national identity any harder. Schools exist because of the need for institutionalised forms of education for children. Faith schools exist because adherents of some faith want their children to receive systematic expert instruction in it which they are unable to supply at home. In the eyes of such parents, religious instruction forms as vital a part of their children's education as anything else taught at school. The faiths that faith schools nurture are not their own creation. It might well be harder for the different institutionalised religions to reproduce themselves across the generations were faith schools no longer able to impart religious instruction and nurturance. But that is no reason to seek their closure on grounds of their divisiveness, unless it is also thought that humankind would be better off dispensing with religion altogether, at least in its institutionalised forms. There are, of course, many who argue this. But equally there are many who think otherwise. For the former to impose their will on the latter would be oppressive in the extreme.

At this point, opponents of faith schools might say that, precisely because of the indemonstrability of the superior merits of any particular faith, the state should not support any variety of faith school. Instead, their argument runs, the state should only fund schools that confine what they teach and their other activities to what is demonstrably of benefit. Should parents wish their children to receive any form of religious instruction, therefore, they should make provision for it elsewhere out of their own resources.

This argument might *seem* compelling, especially to those for whom no form of institutional religion holds any attraction. However, it is open to several major objections. First, the argument assumes that some subjects are so indisputably beneficial as to justify the state demanding that all children should be made to study them. Only such subjects, it might be claimed, should be taught by schools that receive state funding. However, suppose no system of schooling were possible that could teach all these subjects in a way that would enable all children to receive a satisfactory education in them without some of them having to forgo a degree of religious observance that their parents wished them to observe in school. Were the state prepared to fund only such schools, then parents who desired their children to maintain a stricter degree of religious observance than was compatible with their attendance at these state-funded schools would be obliged to pay for their children's education at some suitable independent faith school. However, suppose some of these parents were unable to pay the school fees. One of two things must then happen. Either their children would be kept away from school and thereby denied a proper education, or those children would be compelled to attend schools that would prevent them from observing their faith in a manner their parents would have taught them to consider their religious duty. A state would act unfairly were it to demand that all children receive a basic education in a certain range of subjects, yet was only willing to fund schools that could not meet the religious requirements of some parents who were both able and willing to meet the *extra costs* of suitable faith schools for their children. That unfairness would still remain, even if such parents were able to meet the full costs of independent religious schools for their children.

In order to be able to reach the conclusion that, in a society as religiously diverse as present-day Britain, it would be unjust and oppressive for the state to fund only community schools, there is need of only one further premise. This is the premise that no educational system that consisted of only common schools could avoid obliging some children to abstain from what their parents considered to be essential religious observances. Consider, for example, the logistical problem facing a system of common schools catering for devout Christian, Jewish, Muslim, Hindu and Sikh children and which sought to accommodate all their manifold religious requirements. Not only would the daily school timetable have to take into account all the different times at which studies might need suspending for acts of worship. That might be arranged with some ingenuity. The school calendar would also have to provide sufficient continuity of tuition to all children in all compulsory subjects, whilst simultaneously accommodating the various different times of the school year at which they would be absent for festivals and fasts.

It stretches credibility beyond breaking point to suppose that any system of purely common schools could accommodate the various religious requirements of children of many diverse faith backgrounds nearly as well as a system of schools that included faiths schools. Therefore, suppose a state is willing to make schooling freely available in all subjects whose benefits were considered to be so uncontroversial as to warrant it being made an offence for parents to fail to arrange for their children to study them. Should the state also seek to respect the religious needs and wishes of all religious parents, it will have no alternative but to be willing to fund separate faith schools for all children whose religious requirements could not be accommodated at common schools. This conclusion is subject to two provisos. First, parents of such children, together with their relevant faith communities, must be willing to bear the additional costs of the provision of such schools. Second, all faith schools must provide a satisfactory education in all subjects that are considered so uncontroversial as to warrant the state demanding all children should be made to study them. Moreover, none of these schools should teach anything detrimental to community cohesion.

So far as Britain is concerned, there is a still more compelling moral case that can be made out for the state to provide separate faith schools for the children of all parents whose religious requirements cannot be adequately catered for by community schools. As things presently stand, the education that all community schools are supposed by law to provide is not a purely secular one. All state schools, even community schools, are supposed by law to provide a form of education that includes the study of religion plus a daily act of collective worship that all pupils must attend unless expressly withdrawn by their parents. Moreover, the daily act of collective worship and the religious study in which pupils are meant to engage is supposed to be predominantly Christian, unless parents seek the exemption of their children on conscientious grounds. Where pupils of a community school are predominantly of some other faith than Christianity, then it may seek permission to institute some of form of religious education and assembly better suited to its pupils' affiliations. It follows, therefore, that, as the law currently stands, all children at all maintained schools are supposed to receive a *religious* education. In these circumstances, therefore, it is hard to see how and why the British state could legitimately refuse to fund faith schools for children whose religious requirements cannot be adequately catered for at community schools.

In face of the country's increasing religious diversity, or for other more ideological reasons, many community schools have come to abandon or secularised their religious assemblies. They have also increasingly secularised the study of religion they provide, largely turning it into the comparative study of all the major religions present in Britain today, plus some elementary philosophy of religion and ethics.

In effecting this transformation, community schools in England have over the years been aided and abetted by the Department of Education. It has agreed with and helped propagate a very dubious piece of legerdemain that reinterpreted the relevant sections of the 1988 Education Reform Act in a way manifestly contrary to its original intentions. Since the 1944 Education Act, all schools within the maintained sector have been under a statutory duty to provide a religious education; its Christian nature was taken for granted. Community school were required not to teach denominationally in a way in which voluntary-aided schools had always been permitted. But from the mid-1960s onwards, common schools or 'county schools' as they were then known increasingly began to abandon or secularise their religious assemblies and ceased to teach the non-denominational rudiments of Christianity in a way that presupposed their fundamental truth.

The 1988 Education Reform Act had in part been designed to reverse this trend: first, by requiring all pupils at 'county schools' to take part in a daily act of collective worship that was to be 'wholly or mainly of a broadly Christian character',[1] second by reminding schools of their statutory duty to provide religious education in accordance with a 'locally agreed syllabus'. It further stipulated that, from September 1988, newly agreed syllabuses had to 'reflect the fact that the religious traditions in Great Britain are in the main Christian whilst taking account of the teaching and practices of the other principal religions represented in Great Britain'.[2] Under the Act, community schools could apply to the body that agreed their religious education syllabus, their local Standing Advisory Council on Religious Education or SACRE, for it to reconsider its suitability, as well as to allow it to institute 'alternative collective worship'.

The 1988 Act was expressly designed to ensure that both the religious assemblies and the study of religion at county schools were suitable for their pupils given the faith backgrounds of their families. It had not been intended to require, or arguably even to permit, community schools to incorporate into their religious assemblies elements from all the country's main religions, whilst still giving predominance to Christianity. Nor had it been intended to compel them, or arguably even permit them, to substitute for the teaching of what was expected to be Christianity in most schools the comparative study of all the country's main religions. This is clear from the parliamentary discussions about the relevant sections of the Act before it was made law. In a debate in the House of Lord in June 1988 about the relevant sections of it dealing with religious education, Graham Leonard, then Bishop of London and chairman of the Church of England's Board of Education, clarified the meaning of section 8.3 of the Act that had been introduced as an amendment by Baroness Cox:

> It does not mean that there will be a percentage of Christian teaching spread throughout the country with a proportion of other faiths. It means what it says which is that in the main, looking at the country as a whole with its present multi-cultural composition, the bulk of it will be Christian. The norm will be Christian if one likes to put it that way. But there will be exceptions because of local areas and what is proper to them in the educational setting. This is what we mean by 'mainly'—not 'mainly' in the sense of two-thirds rice and one third tapioca or something like that.[3]

It is the purpose that Christian children should receive teaching in the Christian faith, secondly, it is the purpose that children of other faiths should be taught their own faiths.[4]

Shortly after its enactment, section 8.3 of the 1988 Education Reform Act became subject to a very tendentious reading that reversed this original intent. John Hull, a professor of religious studies at the University of Birmingham and editor of the *British Journal of Religious Education*, wrote a detailed exegesis of section 8.3, jointly published in 1989 by his university and the Christian Education Movement. Hull claimed that what the section really means was that community schools 'will not be meeting the legal standards unless [their pupils] are taught the teaching of the principal non-Christian religions in Great Britain'. Hull's reading of Section 8.3 went unchallenged by the Department of Education which eventually began to endorse his reading of it.

In guidance that it issued to Chief Education Officers in March 1991, as well as in a circular to local education authorities that it issued in January 1994, the by-then DfES advised that religious education syllabuses for use in community schools must neither be based on Christianity alone, nor 'designed to urge a particular religion or religious belief on pupils'.[5] In claiming the latter, the DfES asserted, quite mistakenly, that such a proscription had been imposed by a section of the 1944 Education Act that, in fact, had only forbidden community schools (or county schools) from teaching 'denominational formularies'. This Act had not forbidden such schools from teaching that Christianity was true or from teaching that any other religious was. The DfES admitted their error in a letter that it sent to all SACREs in England after it had been drawn to its attention. However, the DfES continued to stand by its advice that community schools may not teach any religion as being true. This contradicted one case in 1997, when a resident of the Isle of Wight complained to the DfES that a community school had been urging New Age beliefs on his child. The DfES rejected his complaint, stating '*no* religious beliefs urged on pupils would fall foul' of the relevant section of the legislation.[6]

This highlights the injustice of withholding state funding from religious schools that cater to children of religiously-minded parents when community schools do not fulfil their needs. Community schools have always been intended to provide their pupils with some form of religious education and religious belief.[7]

At this point, secular-minded critics of faith schools might respond to this line of argument by saying: so much the worse for current legislation. They might ask why any state-funded schools should be expected or entitled to nurture in their pupils *any* form of religious belief. They would argue that instead state-funded schools in Britain should adopt the American example and offer only a strictly secular form of state schooling.

In response to this suggestion, several points may be made. First, it would, indeed, be wrong for schools to endeavour to nurture in their pupils any form of religious belief that was contrary to the wishes of their parents. Hence, parents must retain the right to withdraw their children from any committed form of religious education or act of worship they consider unconscionable. Equally, as children become older and increasingly more able to decide these matters for themselves, their attendance at any such classes or religious assemblies should become optional.

However, the mere indemonstrability of a given belief, or the irrefutability of one, does not establish that its nurturance in young children is always necessarily pernicious and anti-educational. Of course, any such beliefs should not run contrary to parental preference. Nor should their nurturance be carried out by schools by any pedagogic means other than those deemed suitable for use in teaching other subjects. Subject to these conditions, the mere indemonstrability and irrefutability of beliefs does not establish that their nurturance in school is unjustified. Indeed, if children come from homes in which some religion is being taken seriously and practised, it would arguably be wrong were they not to have the opportunity in school to receive instruction about that religion and to engage in corporate forms of worship according to its liturgy and creed. For primary schools not to reflect and help their pupils learn about the religion practised in their parental home would be profoundly anti-educational. So too, arguably, would their teaching during the early years of schooling about religions other than the one practised at home. To attempt to teach young children about any more religions than their own before they had become conversant with it could only serve to sow seeds of confusion in their minds, both about it and about all other religions. Not only is it unrealistic to attempt to teach young children about other religions before they have become fully conversant with their own; to do so is also subversive of their religious formation.

Doubtless learning about alternative religious points of view is highly desirable at some stage in every child's education. But to embark upon such exposure before children have acquired a firm sense of their own religious identity can be deeply unsettling for them when they come from a home where their religion is taken seriously.

Even children from irreligious backgrounds arguably miss out in their schooling when it is purely secular in character. Provided that their parents have no objections, even such young children might benefit educationally from being made to gain the first-hand experience of elementary forms of religious emotion, such as awe and devotion, which they can be made to do by attending religious assemblies with the liturgy and ritual of which they have become familiar.[8] For their schools not to supply pupils who come from secular homes with the opportunity to experience such emotions is arguably to deny them the wherewithal for being able fully to appreciate any religious works of art of which the greatest constitute a considerable part of the cultural heritage of the West today. They are works with which children should be expected to become familiar at some points in their education, save upon the express conscientious objection of their parents. Likewise, a lack of sympathetically presented instruction in some faith can deprive children from secular homes of the wherewithal later in life of the basis on which to make an informed choice as to whether any particular form of organised religion has something to offer them. The suggestion that, to avoid bias or indoctrination, a child needs instruction in the rudiments of *all* faiths misses the point. For, despite neither being demonstrable nor falsifiable, they are all mutually incompatible. Hence, the potential appeal of more than one of them cannot be adequately conveyed to a child before some one has been given precedence.

What is at issue here is where the default position in schools should lie. Should the committed teaching of religion to children in school be off-limits, unless it has been expressly requested by their parents? Or should schools provide pupils with some committed form of religious education, unless their parents have expressly objected to their children receiving it? Since the 1870 Education Act, Britain has favoured the latter option, even though it was not until the 1944 Education Act that religious education became explicitly mandatory by law in all maintained schools.

Those opposed to the state financially supporting any form of religious education in schools often appeal to how few people in Britain today attend church services on any regular basis or hold any religious beliefs. For example, in November 2001 the *Guardian* published an article by Polly Toynbee entitled 'Keep God out of class'. In it, she stated that: 'at most seven per cent of the UK population go to church, three per cent are devout Muslims or Sikhs... Some 45 per cent of the population has no religious belief'.[9] Critics like Toynbee also like to cite opinion polls that show a majority of those polled to be opposed to the state funding of faith schools. One such poll was commissioned by the *Guardian* shortly after the July 2005 London suicide-bombings. It found that nearly two thirds of those polled agreed that 'the government should not be funding faith schools of any kind'.[10]

These considerations, however, do not carry very much weight in relation to whether the state should fund faith schools or to whether community schools should provide some committed form of religious education, typically some non-denominational form of Christianity, as indeed they are all supposed to. The 2001 Census introduced a new voluntary question asking for the religious affiliations of all individuals resident in every household. Contrary to what Polly Toynbee asserted, the results of the 2001 Census established that the population of Britain remains overwhelmingly religious in orientation, with Christianity by far the most popular faith. According to the Office for National Statistics, the 2001 Census revealed that: 'There were 41 million Christians in 2001, making up almost three quarters of the population (72 per cent)... People with no religion formed the second largest group, comprising 15 per cent of the population. About one in 20 (five per cent) of the population belonged to a non-Christian religious denomination.' [11] These figures match the results of a survey carried out by the *Wall Street Journal Europe* in 2004. It found that: '72 per cent of [Britain's] population believe in some kind of God, while almost as many—69 per cent—associate themselves with a particular religion... 40 per cent of people [in the UK] identified themselves as Protestants, 29 per cent as Catholics and four per cent as Muslims'. [12] The figures are borne out by the results of a telephone poll of over 1,000 respondents conducted for BBC News by ICM in November 2005. Only 22 per cent of those polled described themselves as being of no faith: 'More than two thirds ... said they were Christian. Almost 75 per cent of respondents said the UK should retain

Christian values—including 69 per cent of Jews and nearly 50 per cent of Muslims, Sikhs and Hindus... Some 44 per cent of those who said they had no faith agreed that the UK should retain a Christian ethos.'[13] The figures agree with a 2008 survey carried out by Populus which found that 'two out of three people [in Britain] think that there is still a place for religion in modern life'.[14]

It is unclear against which precise varieties of maintained faith school the *Guardian's* ICM poll in August 2005 showed there to be large-scale opposition. As the head of a mixed Anglican voluntary-aided comprehensive school in Kent pointed out several months later:

> They were perhaps in part voting against a scarcely articulated idea of faith schools as places where children are indoctrinated with fundamentalist and irrational religious beliefs at the taxpayers' expense and then released on an unsuspecting world to become at best religious nutters, and at worst dangerous extremists. Nothing could be further from the reality of what state-funded voluntary aided religious schools do... [T]hey are all obliged to follow the National Curriculum, are all inspected and publicly accountable, and have all recently formally agreed to do what the vast majority have been doing for many years—namely teach children about religions other than their own. The problem is perhaps that the term 'faith schools' has also been applied in the media to privately-funded schools run by various fundamentalist or extreme Christian or Muslim groups and has been confused in the public mind with the religious voluntary aided sector.[15]

Critics of the state-funding of faith schools are still liable to find them objectionable. This is no matter how un-coercive the manner of their nurturance of religious belief might be, and however moderate the form of religion that they nurture. Their critics will still claim such schools to be socially divisive, injurious to the autonomy of their pupils, and vehicles of social privilege, whether by design or accident. These several charges against them remain to be considered. In what follows, however, what will be said by way of their defence will assume the schools in question are indeed moderate. To the extent they are anything other, they should not receive state funding. Nor, arguably, in extreme cases should immoderate schools be allowed to operate at all, even as independent schools.

5

Faith Schools as Agents of Cohesion

No matter how moderate the religious stance of faith schools might be, many of their critics still claim that they are inimical to community cohesion. They do so simply on the grounds that such schools segregate children according to their different family faiths. These critics of faith schools claim that community cohesion demands that children of different faiths be taught alongside each other, or at least at all schools which are funded by the state. This claim about these schools will now be addressed.

It was argued earlier that no system of purely community schools could surmount the purely logistical problem of providing a satisfactory shared form of education for all school-age children, if they were of many different faiths of which the observances were taken seriously by their families. However, for the sake of argument, suppose this problem could be overcome, and that pupils of several different faiths and of none could all be taught together in community schools. Even then, their being co-schooled would not necessarily yield a more cohesive society than would arise from enabling parents to send their children to the faith school of their choice. Those who claim that schools in which children of different faiths are taught together are productive of greater community cohesion than faith schools might like to pretend otherwise. However, as things presently stand in Britain, all too many of its community schools afford pupils far less immunity than faith schools do from bullying and abuse at the hands of children of different ethnicity or faith to theirs. Recent years have witnessed a steep rise in reports of racist incidents in school. Channel Four News discovered this in 2007 through a probe of over 90 local education authorities:

> Cities such as Leeds, Manchester and Birmingham have seen a distinct hike in reported racism in the classroom—prompting fears of a link with perceptions over terrorism... The number of racist incidents recorded in Leeds's schools jumped from 1,142 in 2002/3 to 1,430 in 2005/6. Over the same period Birmingham's schools saw an increase from 832 to 1,577, and Manchester's schools from 590 to 696. Other noticeable rises in racist reports were in Bolton, Coventry, Derby, Dudley, Kent and Lancashire... [R]acist rows rose from 16,251

in 2003/4; to 18,625 in 2005/6... 95,022 have been reported since records began [in most cases, since 2002]. [1]

Some have attributed the increase in racist incidents at school to better reporting techniques. Others disagree, such as Professor Heidi Mirza of London University's Institute of Education. She reacted to the reported increase by saying: 'I think there's a definite problem with racism in schools. I think one of the biggest issues we have is actually under-reporting of these issues'.[2] The Commission for Racial Equality also took the reported increase at face value: 'Worryingly, racist bullying seems to be an increasing and persistent problem in some of our schools. This isn't just a black and white issue, it affects children from all backgrounds, races and religions... Figures show that children from all backgrounds, races and religions, not just Muslims, are suffering at the hands of bullies.'[3]

At the end of February 2008, the British Council published a survey of 3,500 secondary school-age children attending 47 schools across Europe chosen for their mix of children from different backgrounds, including over 1,500 children from the UK. It found:

- Bullying in secondary schools is worse in the UK than the rest of Europe.

  Nearly half of UK secondary schools pupils (46 per cent) think that bullying is a problem in their school and is caused by students' language difficulties, skin colour, race and religion.

- The situation is perceived to be worse in England, where 48 per cent of pupils think bullying is a problem in school, compared to 43 per cent of pupils in Scotland and 32 per cent in Wales.

- Some 41 per cent of respondents said they had been made fun of because of language difficulties, 31 per cent said skin colour, 29 per cent because of racial differences and 27 per cent because of their religion... Some 42 per cent of respondents said it [was] owed to the clothes pupils wear and 44 per cent because of differences in physical appearance.[4]

These statistics make for depressing reading. It would not be extrapolating from them too far to suppose that the incidence of racist bullying and abuse at schools is far higher at community schools than at faith schools, even when the latter are racially mixed. They also suggest that parents who belong to vulnerable ethnic minorities, and whose appearance makes them and their children stand out from others, might have good reason for wanting their children to attend an appropriate faith school rather than a community school. That way their children could avoid the unwanted attentions of fellow pupils with different mother tongues, skin colour, religion or dress.

This consideration is a decisive factor in the choice of faith school for some families. In November 2007, the Runnymede Foundation published the interim results of a 16-month research project that was designed to examine 'how a school system that includes faith schools successfully prepares young people for living in a multicultural society'.[5] To date, over 250 individuals from six different areas in England have contributed their views and experiences in a series of consultations. (The final results of the Runnymede Trust research project were published in December 2008 and its several conclusions and recommendations have been addressed in the Appendix at the end of the present publication.) The interim findings confirm that the protection of their children from bullying lies behind the decision of many religious minority parents to send their children to a faith school. The consultation in Brent and Harrow revealed that: 'Some parents in [North West London] select a Jewish school out of fear of anti-Semitism in other schools'.[6] In Leicester, the consultation revealed that: 'faith schools are often seen as a haven from racism and racist abuse…, mixed-heritage young people [being]… most frequently the reported victims of abuse'.[7] Liverpool is said to have 'the highest proportional representation of faith school (church school) places of any local authority in England'. The consultation there revealed that: 'faith schools were seen by some as a haven from racial harassment and bullying'.[8] The St Anne's district of Southampton is 'a diverse community with 25 languages spoken … particular minority communities are to be found in clusters in certain areas of the city'.[9] The consultation there suggested that 'many Black and minority ethnic students would feel uncomfortable about going to predominantly White estates'. About this suggestion, Audrey Osler, the author of the report, comments: 'it was not clear among those present whether this was a fear based on real threats'.[10] If it was not, then the district of St Anne's would seem to be remarkably immune from a form of social pathology affecting young people today that seems to have reached near epidemic proportions practically everywhere else in the country that has become diverse.

Of course, there are many other reasons why parents might wish to send their children to faith schools besides wanting to spare them from being bullied. For the moment it is enough to note that, arguably, such schools can often serve as sanctuaries from prejudice rather than cauldrons where prejudice is manufactured.

That Muslim children would be spared the risk of being bullied or abused at school by non-Muslim children is one of the main attractions of Muslim faith schools. Certainly, the reported harassment and victimisation of Muslim pupils in non-Muslim schools has been one reason why, over the years, many Muslims have become increasingly disillusioned with community schools. A chapter of Humayun Ansari's book 'The Infidel Within': Muslims in Britain since 1800 is given over to tracing the rise among Britain's Muslims of a movement calling for faith schools of their own. He observed:

> [T]he school social environment also caused concern to many Muslims, especially the harassment experienced by Muslim pupils; evidence from the late 1980s showed how this affected academic achievement. Ahmed Iqbal Ullah's murder in a Manchester school in 1986 by Darren Coulborn, who subsequently boasted 'I've killed a Paki'... gave ample and dramatic illustration of the prevalence of racial abuse and violence in schools and the distress and torment it caused. It revealed too how indifferent and insensitive teachers were to the plight of their pupils...[11]

To spare children from suffering abuse at mixed community schools cannot be considered a dishonourable reason for wanting to establish faith schools, especially when their greater security of children at such schools results in their enhanced academic performance. A case in point is a group of Muslim faith schools established for pupils of mostly Bangladeshi and Pakistani extraction. For a long time, these pupils have been among the least educationally qualified group in Britain. According to the Office for National Statistics: 'In 2003-2004, almost a third (31 per cent) of Muslims of working age in Great Britain had no qualifications—the highest proportion for any religious group.'[12]

Partly, the comparative lack of educational qualifications among members of this group is attributable to many of them being first-generation immigrants to Britain from relatively impoverished peasant backgrounds in the Indian sub-continent where they have had little opportunity for a formal education. However, that is by no means the entire story, as the following statistics reveal: 'In 2000, only 30 per cent of the children of Pakistani and Bangladeshi origin in England and Wales gained five or more GCSEs at grades A*-C, compared to 50 per cent in the population as a whole. This made them the lowest achieving of all ethnic groups... By 2002, the success rate had risen to 40 per cent for Pakistani children and 45 per cent for Bangladeshi children, compared to about 51 per cent for the general population.'[13]

Within this group as a whole, there are very significant internal differences in academic performance masked by the overall aggregate figure. Most notably, Pakistani and Bangladeshi schoolgirls perform *much better* than their male counterparts. In Birmingham in 2003, for example: 'Some 37 per cent of Pakistani boys achieved five or more GCSE passes at grades A*-C, compared to 50 per cent of Pakistani girls; and 43 per cent of Bangladeshi boys achieved the same level, compared to 58 per cent of Bangladeshi girls. The Bangladeshi girls actually exceeded the average for white girls in Birmingham.'[14]

In keeping with what invariably holds true of other faith groups, Muslim students undergo very substantial academic improvement as a result of attending their own faith schools, whether these are voluntary-aided or private. For example:

> [I]n 2001, Islamia Primary School in Brent came third out of 51 schools in the district Key Stage 2 SAT's results, on one measure, and first out of 51, on an adjusted measure. In the 2002 GCSE results, 100 per cent of the pupils entered at al-Furqan Community College in Birmingham, Leicester Islamic academy, Madani School in Tower Hamlets, Tayyibah School in Hackney and Brondesbury College in Brent achieved five or more GCSE passes at grades A*-C... The rate at Feversham College was 53 per cent, slightly above the national average, and well above the [local] Bradford average of 37 per cent. Other Muslim schools, like Zakaria Muslim Girls' School in Batley, have results only slightly lower, and they generally outperform local authority schools.[15]

The reasons why Muslim children of South Asian extraction, especially boys, tend to perform badly in general at school are complex. So too, doubtless, are the reasons for the greatly improved performance of so many of them when they attend a Muslim school. One factor for their improved performance has been their greater freedom from bullying at school by children of other faiths, as argued by Geoffrey Short, Reader in Educational Research at the University of Hertfordshire. Short is author of a pair of articles that jointly offer a robust defence of faith schools against the charge of their being divisive: 'Faith-based schools catering for ethnic minority pupils provide a learning environment that might be seen as contributory in a number of ways to academic achievement. Certainly, the pupils should have to contend with less individual and institutional racism making it easier for them to realise their potential.'[16]

Apart from the lesser likelihood of their being bullied or abused at school due to their race or religion, there are several other possible reasons why pupils from a faith background might perform better at faith schools than at a community schools. First, there is the greater logistical ease of combining religious observance with study. Second, they are more likely to learn about their own faith traditions in such a way as to boost their self-esteem and self-confidence. Third, they are more likely to encounter inspirational role models in the form of charismatic teachers of their own faith with whom they can more easily identify.

By itself, however, enhanced academic performance does not establish faith schools to be as or more conducive to community cohesion than community schools. Establishing this requires showing two things. The first is that faith schools can make some positive contribution towards cohesion that community schools cannot. The second is that no contribution community schools can make exceeds that special contribution faith schools can make.

There is significant evidence in support of both such claims. As regards the first claim, Geoffrey Short has convincingly argued that the greater employability young people acquire as a result of having good educational qualifications shows how an enhanced educational performance at school can promote community cohesion. There is clearly a direct connection between how well children perform academically at school and their future employability. There is also a similar clear positive correlation between a young person's being in employment and the likelihood of their being civil and law-abiding. Because faith schools can typically extract a better academic performance from their pupils than community schools can, it follows that faith schools are able to promote community cohesion in ways in which religiously mixed community schools cannot.

Within recent decades in Britain, there are three groups of pupils with consistently poor academic attainment who consequently suffer high rates of unemployment and economic inactivity. These are Afro-Caribbean males, South Asian Muslim males, and white working-class males. This can be seen from Table 5.1.

As many have pointed out, the only reason that, as a group, white British boys are able to exceed the national average for all boys is by their being pulled up by the much better than average performance of the middle-class ones. Professor Robert Cassen of LSE's Centre for Analysis of Social Exclusion and Dr Geeta Kingdon of the Department of Economics at the University of Oxford found: 'The great majority of low achievers—more than three quarters—are white and British, and far more boys than girls... Nearly half of all low achievers are white British boys... [who] outnumber girls as low achievers by three to two.'[17]

The unemployment rates of the same six ethnic groups in the UK in 1991 and 2001 reveal the correlation between academic attainment and employment (Table 5.2, p. 41).

Table 5.1

Achievements of Boys at GCSE in England in 2007 by Ethnicity

	% Achieving	
	5+ A* to C	5+A* to C incl. Maths and English
Chinese	81.6	66.3
Indian	69.7	56.3
White British	55.2	41.9
Bangladeshi	52.3	36.0
Pakistani	47.0	32.5
Afro-Caribbean	41.5	26.5
All Boys	54.8	41.4

Source: Department for Children, Schools and Families, First Release: National Curriculum Assessment, GCSE and Equivalent Attainment and Post 16 Attainment by Pupil Characteristics, in England 2006/07; 27 November 2007.

The high unemployment rate of the three poorest performing groups of boys has had a predictably adverse knock-on effect upon the cohesion of the low-income neighbourhoods within which they tend to be concentrated. The Social Justice Policy Group states that: 'Almost every symptom of social breakdown is rooted in educational failure.'[18] Their report claimed that three out of four young offenders had no educational attainment, while 37 per cent of adult prisoners had reading skills below those of the average 11-year-old.[19] The high proportion of black and Asian men in UK prisons in 2006, relative to their overall UK population, indicates what a negative impact poor educational attainment must have on community cohesion (Table 5.3).

Table 5.2
Rates of Unemployment and Inactivity among
Males in the UK by Ethnicity

	Unemployment		Economic Inactivity	
	1991	**2001**	**1991**	**2001**
Chinese	11.0	7.0	8.0	11.0
Indian	13.0	7.0	8.0	13.0
White British	10.0	5.0	9.0	14.0
Bangladeshi	29.0	16.0	15.0	20.0
Pakistani	27.0	13.0	13.0	20.0
Afro-Caribbean	23.0	14.0	11.0	17.0

Source: 1991 and 2001 Samples of Anonymised Records, quoted in Clark, K. and Drinkwater, S., *Ethnic Minorities in the Labour Market: Dynamics and Diversity*, Bristol: Policy Press, 2007, p. 4.

Table 5.3
Population in the UK and in prison by self-identified ethnic group

	% of UK Population in 2001	*% of UK prison population in June 2006*
White	91.3	73
Asian	4.7	7
Black	2.8	15

Source: Ministry of Justice, Statistics on Race and the Criminal Justice System – 2006 (London: Ministry of Justice, 2007)

Their lack of employability is liable to have a profoundly deleterious effect upon the cohesion of the communities in which these young men live. Without other sources of self-esteem, they are all too liable to boost it by seeking to gain recognition in anti-social ways that involve ill-treating others. All three groups are tempted to place responsibility for their straightened circumstances upon the shoulders of others. They are thereby easily susceptible to being won over to various forms of extremism. Young white working-class men with few prospects become targets for recruitment by far-right racist organisations keen to ascribe their plight to the excessive power and influence of certain other ethnic groups. Their South Asian Muslim counterparts can easily fall prey to the siren calls of extremist co-religionists keen to ascribe their plight to Western antipathy towards Muslims and their religion. Meanwhile, young Afro-Caribbean men with similarly poor prospects and life circumstances can all too easily become drawn into forms of criminal activity that lead to their imprisonment; some being recruited into militant forms of Islam whilst in prison. Of the 80,000 prisoners in UK prisons in 2006, 11 per cent are estimated to identify themselves as Muslim.[20] Given that Asians formed only seven per cent of the prison population, and few white British men or women have converted to Islam, it follows that a considerable proportion of Muslims in British prisons must be black.

One notorious gang of young Afro-Caribbean men, the so-called 'Muslim Boys', were converted, while in prison, to a form of Islam that made them feel licensed upon release to tyrannise their non-Muslim South London neighbours. According to a report in the *Independent* newspaper from August 2005:

The Muslim Boys have been linked to dozens of murders, shootings and other serious offences in South London in the past 15 months... [A]s soon as the group formed around January 2004, [the Mayor of London's senior adviser on policing] kept receiving consistent reports from members of the black community in Brixton that the gang was not just very well organised but that they would go around and forcibly convert the biggest and brightest of the South-East London criminal fraternity to take up what he terms as a 'criminal jihad'... A [local] resident... and a Muslim himself [who] has grown up alongside a number of the Muslim Boys... says that most of the original group converted while in prison, specifically in Feltham Young Offenders' Institute... He says that for the Muslim Boys, Islam is just another form of shaping a sense of identity and that forced conversions should not be that surprising: 'It's just like any other form of bullying.' [21]

Geoffrey Short suggests how the educational performance, and hence employment prospects, of poorly performing Muslim boys might be improved through forms of schooling that are better adapted to their educational needs than those provided by community schools. The educational needs of South Asian Muslim boys, suggests Short, would be better served by their attending Muslim faith schools. Not only would these schools be likely to enhance the academic performance of these pupils. Assuming such schools taught only some suitably moderate version of Islam, their pupils could also be simultaneously immunised against the possible appeal of extremist versions of Islam which might otherwise prove tempting.

Short also notes that schools that are dedicated to Afro-Caribbean boys might similarly better serve their educational needs. Some might condemn such a suggestion as racist. Yet given his expressed concerns that the country was in danger of 'sleep-walking to segregation', it is pertinent to observe that Trevor Phillips, chair of the Equalities and Human Rights Commission, has been among those who have called for separate schooling for Afro-Caribbean boys.[22] In March 2005, Phillips gave a speech in which he said: 'If the only way to break through the wall of attitude that surrounds black boys is to teach them separately in some classes, then we should be ready for that.'[23]

Short also offers an oblique, but pertinent, suggestion for improving the educational performance of white British working-class boys. It does not involve their being taught separately in white-only faith schools. Rather it involves the re-introduction into the school curriculum of something that has long been denied to such children. This is the wherewithal with which to acquire a sense of their own identity as white and British or English that enables them to feel proud, rather than ashamed, of being such. It is precisely such a sense of their own identities with which Jewish and Muslim children are routinely provided as a result of attending their own faith schools. It is something that they would be far less likely to receive from attending community schools.

Separate *faith* schools were only suggested as a remedy for improving the educational performance of the third poorly performing group: namely, South Asian Muslim boys. That benefit, however, would not by itself be sufficient to demonstrate that such schools were more conducive to community cohesion than community schools. Something else must also be true of faith schools. They must not render their pupils any less able or willing to mix with children of other faiths than they would otherwise tend to be had they been educated at community schools. Given the steep increase in racist incidents reported by schools in recent years, to demand that faith schools met this standard would appear not to impose on them an overly demanding task. However, there are more positive reasons besides the current modest track-record of community schools for supposing that faith schools are every bit as capable as community schools of producing pupils who can and do want to mix with children of other faiths.

In the second of his two articles on faith schools, Geoffrey Short advances both *a priori* arguments and empirical evidence to show that children at them need not be any less able than those at community schools to get on with others.[24] First, he points out, ignorance about the faiths of others need not necessarily result in ill-will towards or prejudices about them. Second, direct first-hand personal acquaintance with members of other faith groups is not the only way in which people of some given faith can learn about these other faiths in ways that leave them well-disposed towards their adherents. This is something, Short points out, that was acknowledged by George Allport, the grand apostle of the contact hypothesis. Short quotes a passage from Allport's classic study on the nature of prejudice in which he observes that: 'There are many ways to impart knowledge about people. One of these is straight academic teaching in the schools.'[25]

To support his contention that faith schools need neither prevent nor disincline their pupils from wanting to mix with children of other faiths, Short cites the results of a three-part ethnographic study that he conducted during 2000 and the early part of 2001. He examined the attitudes and behaviour towards children of other faiths of pupils attending 20 Jewish faith schools in North-West London where 70 per cent of Britain's Jews live. Short interviewed both staff and pupils at a range of different types of Jewish school in terms of their degree of religious orthodoxy. Short's principal finding was that: 'Although many of the children in the survey had received all their formal education in Jewish schools and had been taught little about non-Jewish cultures, almost all of them rejected emphatically the argument that attending a Jewish school makes mixing with non-Jews problematic.'[26] Despite that, and in keeping with what appears a universal trend among human beings, most of these children tended to fraternise outside school *most closely* with those of the same ethnicity as themselves. Despite that exhibited preference, Short found no lack of desire from the majority of pupils to learn more about and to mix more with non-Jewish children:

> '[W]e have lives outside the school. I have a lot of non-Jewish friends and go to a lot of parties with non-Jewish people...' (Sixth form boy)

> 'I seem to get on well enough with non-Jews. I go to dance clubs where 95 per cent are not Jewish and I get on well with them. I also work with people who are not Jewish.' (Sixth form girl)

> 'I have friends who left... and went to a sixth form college and had no problem making friends. Also, I personally don't feel I'll have any problems.' (Sixth form boy)

> 'I've got loads of friends who are not Jewish up my road and when I go on holiday. I make lots of non-Jewish friends.' (Year 6 primary school child);

> 'I have loads of non-Jewish friends. All of my sister's friends are mostly Christian or Hindu or Buddhist and I get on really well [with them].'(Year 6 primary school child).[27]

Faith schools, therefore, do not necessarily impair their pupils' ability or willingness to mix with those of other faiths. Nor are community schools by any means guaranteed to achieve this outcome, as the high rates of racial incidents currently reported by schools show. It may be that, in the interests of greater community cohesion, religious schools that are more conservatively-minded could, and should, do more than they have traditionally been inclined to do to teach their pupils about other faiths. However, there seems no reason to think that they should be made to reserve a certain quota of places for pupils of other faiths. Nor is there any reason to think that faith schools cannot both in principle and in practice be as equally productive of community cohesion as community schools are. Indeed, by being able to enhance the educational performance of their pupils, there is reason to think that, especially in connection with South Asian Muslim boys, faith schools are able to promote community cohesion more effectively than community schools are likely to at least for the foreseeable future.

6

Faith Schools and Pupil Autonomy

Some religiously-minded parents place their children in faith schools that match their own beliefs primarily to spare them from being bullied at community schools. Others do so for the sake of the enhanced educational performances that they seem so routinely able to achieve. Unquestionably, the chief reason that they do is a desire to see their faith transmitted to their children and a belief that it can be far more effectively nurtured in them at a suitable faith school than by any other means. Whether this is grounds to allow them to shall now be considered.

Regardless of whether faith schools are more or less socially divisive than community schools, some of their critics take exception to their endeavours to nurture faith in their pupils, even when undertaken with parental consent or upon their express request. Critics, such as the humanist philosophers quoted earlier, consider the nurturance of religious belief by faith schools to be a form of mental injury inflicted on their pupils; the imposition on their pupils of indemonstrable beliefs and values before they are of an age to decide for themselves whether to embrace them on their merits. Moreover, they argue, these schools typically go about nurturing their favoured beliefs and values in ways that are deliberately designed to shield pupils from giving serious consideration to alternative points of view that could compete for their allegiance, and that might be more suited to their temperament and personality.

The accusation against faith schools, therefore, is that they are deeply anti-educational, their aim being to close the minds of their pupils to any but the beliefs and values of their particular faith. Blind and uncritical acceptance is their goal. In sum, according to these critics, faith schools are intrinsically objectionable since their very mission is to place road-blocks in the way of their pupils' making progress towards intellectual and moral autonomy, whose attainment, they claim, should be the true goal of a liberal education. Even if the law might not prohibit parents from sending their children to such schools, it cannot be a legitimate part of the business of the state to assist in the funding of

46

such schools. How valid is this charge against faith schools and the state funding of them?

On behalf of faith schools, it may be observed that, so long as parents retain the presumptive right and obligation to raise their children, it is entirely unavoidable that their religious outlooks and attitudes will deeply influence those of their children. Where parents take some religion seriously, it is practically unavoidable that their children will acquire its rudiments early in life, and in such an unreflective manner as cannot be considered autonomous. Unless parents are to be forbidden from bringing up their children in a religious manner, it follows that children from religious homes will be likely to start adhering to a religion, and to do so otherwise than as a result of an autonomous decision by them. They will not have been coerced into doing so. But nor will the religious outlook and identity that they form have been the product of any reflective choice on their part, made in awareness of any genuine alternative possibilities.

In this respect, however, the unreflective non-autonomous manner in which young children acquire their rudimentary religious identity from their parents, or guardians, is no different from the manner in which young children acquire every other element of the world-picture that they unreflectively and non-autonomously form. This is a fact about the human condition that is neither alterable nor regrettable. The ethical importance of this fact was given full recognition by the late nineteenth century idealist philosopher, F.H. Bradley, in a classic observation in his book *Ethical Studies*:

> The child is born... not into a desert, but into a living world... He learns... to speak... and... the tongue that he makes his own is his country's language... it carries into his mind... the ideas and sentiments of his... [compatriots], and stamps them in indelibly... The soul within him is saturated, is filled, is qualified by, it has assimilated, has got its substance, has built itself up from, it is one and the same life with the universal life [of his community]... [T]he 'individual' apart from the community is an abstraction... The mere individual is a delusion of theory; and the attempt to realise it in practice is the starvation and mutilation of human nature, with total sterility or the production of monstrosities.[1]

All human beings, in other words, are unavoidably socially-embedded. It is the ineluctable fate of each of them to grow up encumbered by beliefs, values, affiliations and identities that have not been autonomously chosen by them, but absorbed from their familial and social environments. Nor should this fact about them be a matter of regret, even for those who value autonomy and regard its acquisition as the final end of a liberal education.

Unless children could unthinkingly absorb the culture of their surrounding societies as they do, each would be faced at birth with the Herculean task of determining entirely for themselves whatever beliefs, values and aesthetic tastes they were subsequently to acquire. That would vitiate the possibility of human culture or progress. Moreover, in so far as autonomy consists in the self-determination of beliefs, values and attitudes through open-minded critical reflection and enquiry, its attainment by anyone is owed to forms of reasoning and thinking that cannot be acquired in any more autonomous a manner than that by which people acquire their native-language. As Loren Lomasky observes: 'No autonomy that is worth having is forfeited by accepting the given as having legitimate claims on one's efforts. One who is born to a particular family, nation, and religion is not thereby burdened with an anchor restricting his domain of choice but rather is the beneficiary of an inheritance of a manageable number of prospects for fashioning a worthwhile life.'[2]

It thus shows remarkable inattention to the human condition, or else great selectivity of vision, for the Humanist Group of Philosophers to condemn faith schools for nurturing in pupils religious beliefs and values that they acquire non-autonomously. There is simply no way to prevent children so acquiring their initial identity, beliefs and values. To spare young children early initiation into a faith is no less to determine their identities, beliefs and values in a non-autonomous manner than is their early initiation into one. Basil Mitchell underlined this point in an article on 'Being Religiously Educated' written for a Festschrift marking the 175th anniversary of the Church of England's National Society for Promoting Religious Education:

> However much we may have as our ultimate aim a high degree of autonomy, no one can ever achieve it who has not been reared in a firm tradition in the first place. There is no way of avoiding responsibility on this matter. If educators scrupulously refrain from exerting any influence or imparting any bias, the young will not thereby be enabled to escape all influence and bias: they will receive the confused imprint of other agencies... We can try not to influence

them ourselves, but we cannot prevent them from being influenced at all, nor would it help them if we could.[3]

The humanist philosophers might claim that any non-autonomously implanted beliefs and values should be confined to those capable of empirical verification or else which are beyond contention among all educated people, whether religious or secular. However, it is anything but beyond contention between these two latter groups whether children are best served through confining the beliefs and values that are implanted in them to these two categories alone. Committed secular humanists can no more demonstrate to religious believers the superiority of their own attitude towards religions than can religious believers demonstrate the superiority of theirs. Consequently, a state does not assume a posture of neutrality towards religion, should it decline to fund religious schools for the children of those parents who want them and who, together with their faith communities, are willing to bear their extra costs. It adopts a hostile posture. This is because, by refusing to support such schools, the state can only *weaken* the hold religion will have over the children for whom it will have made such forms of schooling unavailable. William Temple, then Archbishop of Canterbury, drew attention to this point during the debates leading up to the 1944 Education Act, the act which made religious instruction and attendance at a daily act of corporate worship mandatory for all pupils at all state-funded schools. Temple observed that when it came to education: 'There is no possibility of neutrality... To be neutral concerning God is the very same thing as to ignore Him... If the children are brought up to have an understanding of life in which, in fact, there is no reference to God, you cannot correct the effect of that by speaking about God for a certain period of the day. Therefore our ideal for the children of our country is the ideal for truly religious education.'[4] Secular humanists cannot claim, therefore, that by not providing children with any form of religious education they are being spared having their beliefs and identity shaped in a non-autonomous fashion. Whatever their schooling, young children acquire their beliefs and identity otherwise than through their freely informed consent.

It is doubtless because the central claims of religion lie beyond the scope of what can be proved or refuted that there is less consensus in the case of religion than there is in the case of mathematics and the natural sciences. However, it does not follow that the acceptance of any religion is always going to be less reasonable or less rational than is agnosticism or the complete rejection of all religions. The existence of God might not be self-evident, demonstrable or empirically verifiable. However, exactly the same can be said about the non-existence of God. Faced by such total epistemic uncertainty, whichever is the right attitude for someone to adopt on this subject might well turn on the consequences of their adopting one attitude or the other. If someone finds that their life makes more sense and its burdens are made easier to bear by supposing that God exists, why should it not be perfectly reasonable and rational for that person to suppose that God does exist? And if it can be perfectly reasonable and rational for someone to suppose that God exists, why cannot it be just as reasonable and rational for such a person to act in ways that they consider to be appropriate or called for in the light of that supposition, for instance, by engaging in acts of worship or prayer? The case for the reasonableness of religious faith in the face of absolute epistemic uncertainty was well put by James Fitzjames Stephen over a century ago:

> What do you think of yourself? What do you think of the world? Are you a mere machine, and is your consciousness, as has been said, a mere resultant? Is the world a mere fact suggesting nothing beyond itself worth thinking about? These are questions with which all must deal as it seems good to them. They are riddles of the Sphinx, and in some way or other we must deal with them. If we decide to leave them unanswered, that is a choice. If we waver in our answer, that too is a choice, but whatever choice we make, we make it at our peril. If a man chooses to turn his back on God and the future, no one can prevent him. No one can show beyond all reasonable doubt that he is mistaken. If a man thinks otherwise, and acts as he thinks, I do not see how anyone can prove that *he* is mistaken. Each must act as he thinks best, and if he is wrong so much the worse for him.[5]

If Stephen's view is correct, then religious belief is no less rational or reasonable than is the absence of such belief. What holds true of the reasonableness of religious belief also holds true in the case of the nurturance of such forms of belief in young children. Whoever has religious belief will naturally want their children to share it too. This fact highlights a second consideration that may be offered on behalf of the state-funding of schools whose religious ethos matches that of the vast majority of their pupils' families. Schools that ignore faith risk creating in their pupils a form of cognitive and emotional dissonance that impedes their educational development. This is especially true of young children starting school who come from homes where religious observance is taken very seriously. The transition from home to school can often be unsettling for young children. The greater is the disjuncture between these two environments, the more unsettling can this time be. It is not, therefore, an idle indulgence for children from such homes to be provided with a suitable form of faith schooling. It is an educational imperative in their case.

The enforced early exposure of all young children to excessive diversity can be educationally damaging. This point has been articulated with great force by Ian MacMullen in a recent book that defends the state-funding of some kinds of faith school against the charge that they necessarily subvert pupil autonomy:

> For the young child of devoutly religious parents, a school with a secular curriculum, diverse membership, and not a whisper of religious reasons in its pedagogical methods of motivation and justification can be a profoundly disorientating place… [I]t is often precisely the total absence of familiar and reassuring religious language and cues and the presence of a large majority of children from families with very different ethical doctrines that threaten to disturb the young child's fragile sense of self. The problem is especially acute for children from strongly religious families because they will be dramatically outnumbered among their peers by children from families that are less devout, are altogether secular, or subscribe to a different religious doctrine.[6]

It is not just because young children are liable to feel uncomfortable or miserable in schools whose ethos does not mirror that of their own homes that it is desirable, wherever possible, that they should be able to attend a school whose ethos does. MacMullen also argues that, particularly in the case of children from devout religious backgrounds, their not being placed in a suitably matching faith school can have a deleterious effect on their potential for autonomy later in life. Drawing on the work of Elmer J. Thiessen, another philosopher to defend faith schools, MacMullen argues that:

> Ethical reasoning is best taught at first within a fairly well-defined ethical system…, [given] the young child's limited cognitive capacities and social or emotional maturity. It is important not to overwhelm young children with the sheer complexity and enormity of ethical disagreement in the world, or even within the confines of a local community in a modern, multicultural, multi-religious society. Confronted by the full extent of ethical diversity, young children are unlikely to be able to grasp its magnitude without giving up altogether on the idea of reasoning about ethical issues… [A] religious primary

school can be the ideal venue in which to encourage an early, limited form of ethical reasoning in the young child of religious parents.[7]

MacMullen points out that by no means all forms of religious schooling are conducive to the development of ethical and intellectual autonomy in their pupils. Hence, if the eventual attainment of autonomy is a goal on a par with the acquisition of literacy and numeracy, the state should not allow religious schools to operate at all, let alone to receive funding from it, unless they provide all the conditions for its eventual attainment. Some contend all faith schools are inherently inimical to the eventual attainment by their pupils of autonomy. But this is just not so. For a school to enable and facilitate its attainment by pupils, it is neither necessary nor desirable that it should altogether abstain from reinforcing any ethical and religious commitments that they might have brought from home. All a school needs to do is to equip its pupils with the cognitive and moral wherewithal to submit their ethical and religious commitments to critical scrutiny. Primary school is not a good stage in a child's education at which to encourage such critical reflection. Secondary school is, particularly in later years.

Religious secondary schools, even very orthodox ones, are as capable as secular schools of providing their pupils with the cognitive and moral wherewithal with which to examine critically their ethical and religious commitments. Equally, secular schools can fail to do so just like some faith schools can. Faith schools typically fail to provide it by confining their curriculum too narrowly and by teaching it in too dogmatic a fashion. They thereby discourage their pupils from ever being able or inclined to question the tenets and values of their faith community, or else their schools penalise them if they begin to. Secular schools in totalitarian societies can be equally as guilty of stultifying their pupils' autonomy, by teaching an official state ideology in a way that neither encourages nor brooks any dissent. Within liberal secular democracies, there is another more likely reason why some secular schools fail to provide their pupils with these powers of critical examination. They do this by inculcating in pupils, whether intentionally or inadvertently, a form of ethical relativism or indifferentism that disinclines them from questioning whatever ethical commitments they might have unreflectively absorbed from their surroundings. Coming to believe everyone equally entitled to their own opinion and everyone's opinion equally valid, such pupils can all too easily become disinclined from ever wanting to question the ethical commitments or lack of commitments of anyone, including their own.

Both a close-minded dogmatism that refuses even to *consider* alternative points of view, and a hang-loose ethical indifferentism that considers all points of view equally valid, are inimical to personal autonomy. The former will not countenance critical reflection; the latter refuses to engage in serious critical reflection. Schools, in any decent society, should combat both postures. Why exactly? The basic reason is that no basic education can be considered complete that does not acquaint its recipient with at least some of the best of what has been thought and accomplished by humankind in the spheres of art, music, literature and philosophy. Now, it is precisely with ethical commitments, their clashes and the various problems involved in trying to live up to them, with which the greatest works of human culture almost always invariably deal. Hence no form of education that acquaints its recipients with a range of such works can avoid making those recipients of it take ethical commitments seriously. Hence, it is not possible to provide children with a full decent basic education without also necessarily obliging them to take ethical commitments seriously. But any such serious engagement with ethical commitments will invariably involve those who undertake it in having to reflect critically on the ideas and values that they will have unreflectively acquired at home or in their earlier schooling. Exposure to a range of such works of high culture need not necessarily alienate children from such antecedent ethical and religious commitments. They may well end up endorsing them still more strongly in some form as a result of such critical reflection. Such exposure will, however, have obliged them to take ethical commitments seriously, as well as to regard such commitments as not being all of equal validity. It will likewise preclude them from harbouring any unthinking form of dogmatism. A full basic education, therefore, need not destroy religious orthodoxy, only make it informed.

7

Faith Schools and Fairness

Before the state funding of faith schools can be said to have been fully vindicated, it is necessary to meet one more charge that has been levelled against them. This is the charge that, by selecting pupils on the basis of their parents' avowed religious commitments, faith schools disadvantage children coming from less privileged backgrounds. They are said to do so because the parents of the least advantaged children are least likely to avow any such commitment or else be sufficiently savvy and interested in their children's education as to be ready to feign one. Consequently, their children are least likely to gain a place at a faith school and so tend to end up at low-achieving community schools. The children of better-heeled, sharper-elbowed parents, by contrast, tend to end up together at faith schools of one form or another. It is the greater educability of such children, plus the beneficial peer-effect that their presence in large number in schools has on other pupils, that allegedly accounts for why faith schools generally outperform community schools in league tables, not the religious ethos, according to their critics. Were the admissions policies of faith schools changed so that they could no longer 'cherry-pick' the more docile middle-class children, then less advantaged children would benefit. First, places at these schools would become more available to them. Second, local community schools would become more heavily populated by the children of middle-class parents who would spread the benefits of their greater docility more evenly and fairly to those from other back-grounds.

Several studies claim to show underprivileged children to be under-represented in faith schools. One such study, commissioned by the Joseph Rowntree Foundation and conducted by three members of the Education Research Group at the London School of Economics, tried to ascertain 'the religious composition and admissions policies of publicly-funded secondary schools in London'.[1] Published in May 2007, it claimed that two of its findings showed the admissions policies of faith schools were unfair to children from less advantaged backgrounds. First, pupils admitted to voluntary-aided secondary schools were found to have entered with higher levels of prior attainment than those admitted to schools whose admissions policies were under local authority control. Second, fewer children at voluntary-aided schools were found to be eligible for free-school meals, or to have special educational needs, than those at other sorts of maintained schools. Eligibility for free-schools meals is a sign of low parental income and is an accepted measure of how many children at a school come from a disadvantaged socio-economic background. The principal recommendation made by the authors of the report was that: 'if community cohesion is to be fostered, schools with a religious character should be inclusive of all religions (or no faith)'.[2]

A month later, the Institute for Public Policy Research published a second damning report on the selective admissions policies of faith schools: 'The existence of peer effects is perhaps the most important fairness issue in relation to the admissions system. It demonstrates that the selection and segregation of high-ability pupils into specific schools simultaneously improves their chances of further high attainment while damaging the chances of those pupils left behind.'[3] It claimed this peer-effect had been unfairly confined to more socially advantaged children by faith school admission policies. These allowed faith schools, when oversubscribed, to give priority to children whose parents avowed affiliation to their faith. It claimed that such schools were 'hugely over-represented in the top 200 comprehensive schools as measured by examination results... [and] highly unrepresentative of the postcode sector in which they are located'.[4] Only 5.8 per cent of their pupils were eligible for school meals against 13.7 per cent of pupils in local neighbourhoods. The report recommended that maintained faith schools should cease to be allowed, if over-subscribed, to give priority to those of their faith. Instead, every faith school, as with all other maintained schools, should use 'fair-banding by ability as an over-subscription criterion... so that its spread of ability is representative of a wider population'.[5] That wider population could either be all school applicants or else the whole pupil population in an area, such as a local education authority or the country as a whole. To require faith schools to adopt such admissions policies would end their ability to preserve their religiously exclusive character, and thereby their ability to cherry-pick the more educable middle-class children.

How might faith schools meet the accusation that they cream off the more educable children who tend to come from better-off homes, and thereby unfairly disadvantage those who come from less well-off backgrounds?

One possible response to this accusation is to observe that, if there is over-demand, the most obvious remedy is to expand and open more faith schools rather than, as the IPPR report proposed, reduce the availability of places at them for pupils of the faith that they were founded to nurture. Critics of faith schools might respond by claiming that, in the case of over-subscribed Anglican and Roman Catholic schools, the faith commitment of many parents who apply for places is only feigned, not genuine. It is feigned precisely to secure places for their children at these schools. Often cited in evidence of such a claim is the large increase in the number of baptisms that have been carried out on children over the age of one year in recent years by both the Anglican and Roman Catholic churches. Traditionally, these churches have tended to baptise children before that age. The suggestion is that religiously uncommitted parents have been increasingly requesting baptisms for their children only to secure a place for them at an Anglican or a Catholic school. Thus, whereas in 1958 fewer than six per cent of baptisms into the Roman Catholic Church were conducted on children aged over one year, in 2005 that figure had risen to over 30 per cent. Likewise, the number of late baptisms carried out by the Anglican Church rose from 35,000 in 1990 to 39,000 in 2005.[6]

Some of these late baptisms have undoubtedly occurred as part of an attempt by the parents of the children in question to secure a place for them at a religious school. However, the Roman Catholic Church has not been unduly concerned about their increase. One spokesman reportedly commented in response: 'It is not easy to remain a Catholic for long if you are not authentic.'[7] Others have responded with unmitigated pleasure. Oona Stannard, director of the Catholic Education Service for England and Wales, said in January 2008: 'That the child is brought into the Church and the family's bond with the Church strengthened can only be a good thing, irrespective of whether the child does eventually have the benefit of attending a Catholic school.'[8] This seems a perfectly reasonable reaction. After all, these schools exist to nurture the Catholic faith in Catholics. If the prospect of their being able to attend a Catholic school causes a lapsed Catholic to baptise their child, then Catholic schools are fulfilling part of their mission. The same might also be said of Anglican schools when children are made to undergo late baptism by the Church of England for the sake of becoming eligible for a place at an Anglican school.

That reply still does not meet the claim that faith schools unfairly penalise children from disadvantaged backgrounds who are unable to attend them under current admissions policies. Some will still claim that faith schools unfairly deprive these children of the beneficial effects of the presence in class of more educable children who come from more advantaged backgrounds. In response to this claim, the following three points may be made.

First, it is not clear that, on the whole, faith schools discriminate directly or indirectly against children from low income families or who have special needs. As the then Minister for Schools, Jacqui Smith, stated in a Parliamentary debate on the subject in February 2006:

> It is not statistically the case that there are large discrepancies in the social make-up of faith schools as compared to non-faith schools. For the most disadvantaged schools—those with more than 21 per cent of their children receiving free school meals—the proportion of voluntary-aided and other schools is broadly similar. The average free school meal rate in the two categories is broadly similar. In voluntary-aided schools it is 33.8 per cent, whereas in non-voluntary-aided schools it is 34.1 per cent.[9]

There simply was no significant difference in the proportion of disadvantaged children attending voluntary-aided faith schools by comparison with those at other sorts of maintained school. Moreover, voluntary-aided faith schools also benefit pupils from disadvantaged backgrounds when they attend in large numbers. Amongst the most disadvantaged schools, those which are also faith schools generally achieve better examination results. As Jacqui Smith observed: 'It appears from the achievement levels in those equivalent most disadvantaged schools, that despite those similarities voluntary-aided schools are making an important contribution for disadvantaged pupils: 47.6 per cent of pupils in voluntary-aided schools achieve five or more GCSEs at A* to C grade, compared with 40.6 per cent in non-voluntary-aided schools.'[10] Assuming it reliable, what this last statistic arguably shows is that it is not simply peer-effect that accounts for the better performance of children who attend faith schools. It is something else that is more integral to the character and ethos of these schools.

Second, it might well be that, in London and other large cities, faith schools do not always contain as large a proportion of disadvantaged pupils as the population of their neighbourhoods. However, this does not necessarily mean that these schools were discriminating against disadvantaged children, directly or indirectly. Ian Bauckham, head of a religious comprehensive situated in Kent, has said:

> Faith schools tend to draw from much wider catchments than other comprehensive schools, which are often tied to a relatively restricted geographical area. While a [non-religious] comprehensive situated in a leafy suburb is likely to have only a small proportion of underprivileged children, a church school in the same location is much more likely to have children from a distant estate and a much less privileged background.

> This phenomenon is evident in many Catholic schools in our major cities, where a much greater diversity of ethnic groupings drawn from a wide area can be found... than in non-religious comprehensives. The most prestigious of the latter can often be accessed only by those families able to afford high house prices in an immediate catchment area. There is actually a far greater proportion of black African and Caribbean children in Anglican schools nationally than in non-faith schools.[11]

It is not just in leafy suburbs that religious secondary schools often admit a higher proportion of children from disadvantaged backgrounds than community schools. In 2007, one Anglican school, among London's 40 most advantaged schools, still had as many as forty per cent of pupils with free school meals.[12]

Meanwhile, 'the most outstandingly effective secondary school in England' in terms of 'added-value' is Yesody Hatorah, an ultra-orthodox 'Charedi' Jewish comprehensive school situated in Stamford Hill, London.[13] Most of its pupils come from local Charedi families who are typically on very low incomes. A household survey of Charedi families carried out in 2001 found that '62 per cent received child benefits, 70 per cent received housing benefits and 18 per cent received income support'.[14]

Finally, it is not clear that, were all maintained schools to adopt the admissions policies that the IPPR report recommended, children from disadvantaged backgrounds at community schools would necessarily gain the benefit of any peer effects from the greater presence in their schools of more educable middle-class children. A study was recently carried out by several professors of education at a variety of English universities of the progress made at school by 123 children of 'white, urban, middle-class parents who consciously chose for their children to be educated at their local state secondary, whatever the league table positioning'.[15] The children in question were found to have done extremely well: 'Most children who had this choice made for them have gone on to perform brilliantly in GCSEs, A-levels and then on to university entrance, including a much higher than average entry to Oxbridge'. Apparently, however, the other pupils at the 'average or poorly performing schools in working-class or racially mixed areas' attended by these high-achieving middle-class children derived little benefit from their presence at the same schools. The researchers found 'segregation within [these] schools, with white middle-class children clustered in top sets, with little interaction with children from other backgrounds'.

In light of this research finding and of all the others discussed, we may safely conclude that the selective admissions policies of faith schools, in so far as they have any, do not work to the overall disadvantage of children coming from the least advantaged socio-economic backgrounds. In arriving at this conclusion, we complete our examination of faith schools and the several charges levelled against them.

8

Interim Conclusions

The discussion so far has tried to ascertain how far faith schools, whether state-maintained or independent, may justifiably be considered to undermine, or conversely to strengthen, social cohesion in Britain today. Occasioning this enquiry has been the widely canvassed claim that all such schools without exception militate against social cohesion. Some argue that by segregating children along religious lines for purposes of schooling, such schools thereby discourage their mutual contact. Others base their claim on the negative effects of faith schools on social cohesion and the selective admissions policies they are allowed to adopt, enabling middle-class children to cluster in such schools to the alleged detriment of children from less advantaged backgrounds.

These charges were examined and found lacking. Segregation in school along faith lines is not necessarily subversive of social cohesion. Indeed, to the contrary, by enhancing the educational performance of children from disadvantaged religious minorities more than community schools, faith schools might actually be able to play a uniquely important positive role in strengthening social cohesion. They would be able to do so upon the not unreasonable assumption of there being a strong positive correlation between employment and social integration. Equally, the accusation was found to be unsound that faith schools undermined social cohesion by perpetuating and exacerbating class differences.

Whilst exonerated of general charges against them, it cannot be denied that some faith schools do give legitimate cause for concern on grounds of their seemingly negative potential impact upon social cohesion. Within a religiously plural society, few institutions would appear more able to undermine cohesion than faith schools that nurtured within their pupils forms of religious belief that encourage them to hate or feel contempt for others. The only schools that seem to fit this category are a small number of Muslim schools. A great many Muslim schools in Britain cannot remotely be accused of falling into this category. Some, however, appear to. Compounding such legitimate concerns has been the apparent ease with which some of these schools have been able to undergo inspection without their divisive pedagogy being detected, or, if detected, without these schools being forced to revise their pedagogy or close. Their seeming ability to do so reveals the inadequacy of the current inspection regime and the urgency of the need for its review and strengthening. Certainly, Ofsted's recent delegation of responsibility for the inspection of independent Muslim schools to a new inspectorate for them seems a move in precisely the opposite direction. As things presently stand, the country appears to be without remedy against the toxin of sectarian hatred such schools can introduce into the body politic.

Our enquiry also reveals a need to ensure faith schools promote social cohesion. We can say, with some justification, that *all* maintained schools in Britain can legitimately be considered faith schools. This is because they are still required by law to provide a daily act of collective worship as a well a form of religious education that, when it was made a legal obligation, was clearly intended to nurture in their pupils *some* form of religious faith. Today, both these statutory requirements are often honoured more in the breach than in the observance. Moreover it is open to question how reasonable or realistic it is to expect all maintained schools to fulfil them, given how religiously diverse and secular Britain has become. Yet, if rightly handled, discharging this duty could provide even community schools today with a valuable opportunity to engage in forms of pedagogy and corporate activity that could strengthen social cohesion more than current policy has achieved.

As from September 2007, all maintained schools have been placed under a statutory duty to promote community cohesion. How this could be achieved is the focus of the second part of this study.

Part Two:

Country, Classrooms and Cohesion

9

The Government's Community Cohesion Agenda—the Making of a Legend

Ever since a series of disturbances in Bradford, Burnley and Oldham in the summer of 2001, it has been a constant theme of all Government reports about community cohesion that there is a need for people from different backgrounds to have greater contact and to learn more about each other. The Government has gone out of its way to claim Britain's social cohesion is seriously threatened by a lack of such contact and knowledge to redress which requires major initiatives and changes on the part of local authorities and state schools. Underlying the Government's strategy, however, there lies no substantial body of empirical evidence, but rather an ideological agenda that goes by the name of 'Interculturalism'. As we shall now see, it is an agenda that fits almost too comfortably Groucho Marx's satirical description of politics as 'the art of looking for trouble, finding it everywhere, diagnosing it incorrectly and applying the wrong remedies'.

Undoubtedly, the last decade has witnessed a growing militancy incubating within certain sections of Britain's Muslim community. Similarly, following the events of both 9/11 and 7/7, there have been more reported attacks on Muslims. However, as shall be argued below, reports that Britain has suffered a major breakdown in social cohesion are greatly exaggerated. The Government seems to have created a moral panic on this issue. Possibly it has done so in order to avoid having to confront the very real and more specific problems of growing militancy and disaffection among parts of the Muslim community. Instead of directly addressing these problems, it has diverted public attention and dissipated its energies by seeking to address more general, but largely fictitious, problems within which it has subsumed the real ones. As a consequence, the Government has introduced unnecessary innovations into the school curriculum as well as into other areas of social life. As often as not, these innovations have only stoked up resentment among many sections of British society. Rather than forever preoccupying itself with ever more new initiatives to strengthen community cohesion, a strong case exists for the Government seeking to do less, but to focus its efforts more effectively.

Community cohesion has preoccupied politicians, policy-makers, and pundits in Britain ever since the disturbances in Bradford, Oldham and Burnley in the summer of 2001. In all three towns, the overwhelmingly majority of the rioters were young male Muslim residents of South Asian extraction. Whatever had led them to riot, their having done so was widely interpreted as being symptomatic of a serious, more general deterioration in relations between the Muslim and non-Muslim (largely white working-class) residents of those towns.

Four years after these riots in July 2005, London's transportation system was the chosen venue for two sets of carefully planned and coordinated suicide-bombings: the first lethally successful; the second, mercifully, not. Again, in both cases, the perpetrators were young Muslim men of mainly South Asian extraction, nearly all of whom had been born and raised in Britain. Further planned, but foiled, attacks and plots warn of still more devastating acts of mass slaughter to follow, unless a way can quickly be found to bring Britain's fast growing Muslim population into closer harmony with their non-Muslim compatriots.

Following the riots of the summer of 2001, central and local government were quick to commission a series of reports to identify their causes. The two best known and most influential of these reports were those produced under the chairmanship of Ted Cantle and John Denham. Another pair were published at the same time and each focused on one of the towns affected by riots. They were commissioned by their borough councils. One was about the causes of the Oldham riots and produced by a team under the chairmanship of Sir David Ritchie. The other report had looked at the disturbances in Burnley and was produced by a team led by Lord (Tony) Clarke. The reports of the teams led by Cantle and Denham took a more synoptic view of the riots than did the reports of the groups led by Ritchie and Clarke, seeking to identify their common causes. The conclusions of both these more general reports were heavily influenced by the content of a fifth report that was released in the immediate wake of the riots but had been commissioned and written beforehand. It was about the cause of the poor state of race relations in Bradford and was commissioned by the town's borough council. It was produced by a group chaired by Sir

Herman Ouseley, a former chairman of the Commission for Racial Equality. Henceforth, each report will be referred to by the surname of the chairman of the team that produced it.

The main question that Ouseley addressed was why community fragmentation had been occurring along social, cultural, ethnic and religious lines in the Bradford District.[1] The report placed the blame squarely upon a self-reinforcing cycle of steady disengagement that it claimed had taken place among the town's different ethnic groups. As each group withdrew from the others, so it claimed, their members became ever more mistrustful of and antagonistic towards those belonging to other groups. This was because their widening separation had deepened their mutual ignorance, thereby, allowing mutual prejudices and negative stereotypes of each other to flourish. The first paragraph of the first chapter of Ouseley opens with the following unequivocal declaration:

> Communities are fragmenting along racial, cultural, and faith lines... Rather than seeing the emergence of a confident multi-cultural district, where people... have understanding and tolerance for differences, people's attitudes appear to be hardening and intolerance towards differences is growing. This situation is hindering people's understanding of each other and preventing positive contact between people from different communities.[2]

Ritchie and Clarke advanced similar explanation for the poor state of inter-communal relations in Oldham and Burnley which they claimed had been ultimately responsible for the riots they had suffered. Ritchie spoke of the emergence within Oldham of 'a system of separate development... in which people from different ethnic backgrounds live largely separated from one another'.[3] It also claimed that: 'Bangladeshis and whites simply do not meet one another to any significant degree, and this has led to ignorance, misunderstanding and fear...[4] One of our most important conclusions has been the lack of opportunity for people to meet and talk across the community divides...[5] People must come together much more than has happened recently in Oldham...'[6] As a consequence, there was need for much greater residential, educational, and social mixing on the part of Oldham's different ethnic groups: 'Older people have a big responsibility to understand one another better, and to break down their stereotypes'.[7]

Clarke spoke of Burnley in similar vein, noting 'a high level of prejudice, ignorance and misunderstanding about other cultures within the Borough'.[8] That alleged high level of mutual prejudice among Burnley's different ethnic groups was attributed to their lack of contact: 'There are, in fact, very few opportunities for most of Burnley's white and minority ethnic groups to mix and understand each other's cultures...[9] Communities are divided and do not mix together either socially or in terms of service provision... The lack of awareness of others... has led to an exacerbation in the levels of distrust and misunderstanding between Burnley communities.'[10]

Both the Clarke and Ritchie reports claimed that a lack of interaction between different groups of residents had fostered mutual prejudices and mistrust, and that these had fuelled the animosities that lay behind the disturbances. Given how heavily Cantle and Denham both drew on these two reports and on the Ouseley report, it was unsurprising that they should have echoed these same themes. Cantle: 'While the physical segregation of housing estates and inner city areas came as no surprise, the team was particularly struck by the depth of polarisation of our towns and cities... Separate educational arrangements, community and voluntary bodies, employment, places of worship, language, social and cultural networks, mean that many communities operate on the basis of a series of parallel lives... There is little wonder that the ignorance about each others' communities can easily grow into fear.'[11] Denham: 'We recognise that in many areas affected by disorder or community tensions, there is little interchange between members of different racial, cultural and religious communities and that proactive measures will have to be taken to promote dialogue and understanding...'[12]

The Government's entire community cohesion agenda has been predicated upon the validity of the common analysis that all five reports gave of the source of the inter-group tensions underlying the summer 2001 disturbances. The reports all attributed the disturbances ultimately to a lack of contact between different groups which generated poor mutual relations. But is that analysis of the cause of the disturbances warranted?

Nowhere did any of these five reports offer any evidence on behalf of their common claim that the July 2001 disturbances were due to the poor state of relations between the different groups of residents of the towns in which they had occurred, and that these poor relations had been caused by a lack of contact. This officially received explanation of the cause of the riots is open to serious doubt. There is an alternative, much better grounded explanation of the disturbances that all five reports assiduously avoided considering.

In order to see what is wrong with the officially received explanation of the riots, there is need to appreciate several important facts. The first is that, contrary to the claims of all five reports, in the decade before the riots took place there not been any increasing self-segregation on the part of their different ethnic groups. During this period, the size and density of the South Asian Muslim populations of certain districts of these towns had certainly increased. However, to attribute that increase to the self-segregation of Muslims and to the deliberate flight of non-Muslims from proximity to Muslims is to imply that increasing numbers of both groups had deliberately chosen to live apart. That simply had not happened.

Very crudely put, 'white flight' from these districts does not account for the increased size and density of their South Asian Muslim populations during the preceding decade. Nor did that increase occur through South Asian British Muslims moving into these districts either from other districts in these towns or from elsewhere in Britain less densely populated by fellow Muslims. The increase in the size and density of the South Asian Muslim populations was the product of two other, far more innocent, demographic factors. The first was simply the very rapid natural increase of their South Asian Muslim populations, an increase due simply to their very high rate of fertility, combined with the arrival of large numbers of foreign immigrants from South Asia who had settled there as a result of family reunion, especially trans-continental arranged marriages.

The second factor contributing to the increased density of the South Asian Muslim populations of these districts was the decline in the size of their white populations over the previous decade. Reasons for that decrease do not constitute 'white flight' in the sense of a deliberate attempt on the part of their white residents to move away from Muslims. First, the fertility rate of the white residents had fallen to below replacement level. More white residents were dying as a result of aging than were having babies. Second, there is a tendency, universal amongst people, to move with growing affluence from poorer inner city areas to outer suburbs and the surrounding countryside. During this period, this same tendency had been as much in evidence among the more upwardly mobile South Asian Muslim residents of these districts as it had been among the white ones.

As a matter of fact, for ten years before 2001 there had been a decline in the degree of segregation of Britain's Muslim population. An increasing number and an increasing proportion of them had moved from inner-city areas of traditional Muslim settlement into areas where the density of Muslims had previously been low. By analysing the results of the 2001 Census and other official data, the demographer Ludi Simpson has shown that, in the years preceding the 2001 census, there had not been any increased self-segregation by Britain's Muslim and non-Muslim populations, either in the three towns in which riots occurred in 2001 or anywhere else:

> Increasing residential segregation of South Asian communities is a myth... South Asian population growth alone has added to existing areas of settlement; more localities have become mixed, more have a South Asian majority and fewer are predominantly White. This change is a result of growth in the South Asian population, not of segregation. [13]

Simpson has also pointed out: 'surveys of households... repeatedly find that many South Asians, particularly young adults, would like to move, with others, to areas outside current settlements'.[14] By analysing the very comprehensive data available for the Bradford District, what Simpson has shown is that: 'the number of majority South Asian areas... increased due to a growth in population from [foreign] immigration and from natural increase, but not from movement of South Asian residents towards areas of South Asian concentration. Demographic evidence shows dispersal, supporting the survey evidence of a desire to live in mixed neighbourhoods by most in the South Asian populations.' [15]

Such revealed and expressed preference on the part of Bradford's Muslim residents is not indicative of any overall deterioration in their relations with non-Muslims. What is indisputable, however, is that, during the decade before the 2001 riots, certain elements within the Muslim populations of these three towns had become increasingly radicalised along religious lines. At the same time, those elements became increasingly hostile towards their non-Muslim neighbours. However, the case is very weak for attributing their increased radicalisation and militancy to any lack of contact with their non-Muslim neighbours. That case is weak because, during the same period, relations between the other ethnic groups resident within all three towns suffered no similar deterioration, despite their not having had appreciably greater mutual contact than had the Muslim residents of these towns with their non-Muslim residents.

This growing radicalisation and militancy of certain elements of the Muslim populations of these towns could well account for why so many young Muslim residents had been predisposed to join in those riots. None of the official reports produced in their wake, however, chose to explore the possibility that these factors might have been among their most important contributory causes. Cantle demurely alludes to the possibility by euphemistically noting that 'most of the disturbances have involved youths of Pakistani origin and this seems to point to a growing disaffection, related to changes within their community'.[16] However, in so far as Cantle cites the rioters' religious beliefs as having been a contributory factor, it does so only by suggesting that local Muslims had fallen victim to 'Islamophobia': 'Islamophobia was also identified as a problem in the areas we visited and for some young people was part of their daily experience... It is not simply a coincidence that the Pakistani community were, principally, at the centre of the disturbances.'[17]

Including the religion of the rioters among the contributory factors in this way suggests that, at worst, they had merely been reacting against animosity directed at them. Undoubtedly, local Muslims had been targeted by orchestrated far-right violence and intimidation. Yet to suggest this was the only way in which their religion had been implicated in the riots overlooks the substantial body of evidence of previously mounting religious sectarianism, fuelled by the increasing radicalisation of many young local Muslims. During the decade before, all three towns in which riots took place, plus several adjacent ones, had witnessed a growing militancy on the part of many young Muslim residents. This militancy had been directed at all non-Muslims in those towns, not just against the white far right, as Anthony McRoy has demonstrated in his carefully documented account of the period.[18] Hindu, black and, South Asian Christian residents of these towns had all been subjected to Muslim violence and intimidation. Even Ahmadiyyas had suffered attacks at the hands of Muslims, being a Muslim sect whom many other Muslims regard as heretics. Such Muslim militancy can hardly be described as having been a reaction to far-right white 'Islamophobia'. For, during this period, increasing numbers of Muslims in these towns were made hostile towards *all* who were not of their own religion, not just towards whites.

Anthony McRoy has documented various incidents of local Muslim militancy towards non-Muslims that strongly suggest the cause was more than prejudices and negative stereotypes borne of mutual lack of contact between groups. He quotes a letter published by the *Guardian* in May 2001 written by a Pakistani Christian about 'a mini ethnic cleansing' in Oldham that had gone on for the previous three years 'encouraged by mullahs from mosques'.[19] The letter stated that: 'Young Muslims have been encouraged to attack Hindu homes and shops' and also claimed that, in 1999, 'the Diwali lights in a Hindu enclave [had been]... torn down and destroyed by Muslim thugs'.[20]

McRoy also points out that Ritchie had denied claims that local Muslims in Oldham had created no-go areas there, despite testimony to the contrary from local residents. In April 2001, a young Muslim resident from Oldham's largely Muslim Glodwick estate had claimed in an interview on BBC Radio 4 *Today* programme that: 'there are signs all around saying whites enter at your risk'. Similarly, the Labour MP for Bradford South had said that 'there is a core of people... who want to create no-go areas'.[21]

McRoy then turns to Clarke and to how it had focused exclusively on the preaching of hatred and prejudice by white racist groups in Burnley. This is despite it having been widely known locally that, in 2000, a chapel there and its congregation had been subjected to a protracted campaign of vandalism and intimidation by Muslims who had wanted its land on which to build a mosque. It was also despite the broadcast in 1999 of footage of a sermon delivered at a mosque in Burnley by Abu Hamza in which he had called on his audience 'to learn martial arts, disguise themselves, and to "rip the intestines" out of local infidels!'[22] BBC radio had broadcast a programme about similar attacks on churches and church officials in Bradford during this period, although no mention of these attacks was made in any of the reports about the disturbances.[23]

McRoy suggests that the growing radicalisation and militancy during this period of many young British Muslims was 'ultimately... the result of perceived government insensitivity to Islamophobia since the Rushdie crisis of 1989, as well as of British foreign policy in the

Middle East and especially its perceived negative role during the Bosnian conflict'.[24] Whether that is so, what seems especially hard to credit is that such growing militancy on the part of many Muslims was mainly caused by their lack of contact with non-Muslims. This is especially so, given how well integrated each of the four 7/7 suicide-bombers had apparently been before their radicalisation.

It is no small matter whether the officially received explanation of the 2001 riots is correct. The entire country's education system is currently in process of major overhaul on the basis of its being supposed that community cohesion requires the engineering of much greater contact between groups than would otherwise occur spontaneously. Their increased contact is being engineered by the state on the basis of its being supposed that it was a lack of contact between different groups that caused the poor inter-communal relations that were exhibited by the 2001 disturbances in Oldham, Burnley and Bradford. But what if that was not their real explanation?

10

The Contact Hypothesis Examined

In attributing the inter-communal disturbances to a lack of contact between the different groups of residents of the towns in which they occurred, all five official reports seem to have drawn heavily on a very well-known, but highly disputed, theoretical paradigm for understanding ethnic conflict without acknowledging that they had. This theoretical paradigm has been dubbed *the contact hypothesis*. It was first so named by George Allport in his classic text of 1954, *The Nature of Prejudice*, a book that did much to popularise the notion.[1]

In its crudest version, what is asserted by the contact hypothesis is that, where different ethnic groups have previously enjoyed little contact on an equal-status basis, each group will be liable to acquire and harbour prejudices and negative stereotypes of the other group that will prevent their members from getting on. The quotations from the five reports offered earlier make it clear that they had all assumed the validity of the contact hypothesis. None, however, cites any evidence for it. Nor do any of them indicate where such evidence might be found. The validity of the hypothesis has been taken for granted in all subsequent official Government literature on community cohesion, and it has effectively become the cornerstone of its entire community cohesion agenda. This agenda seeks to promote community cohesion by fostering greater contact between groups who come from different backgrounds. None of the official Government literature on community cohesion to have appeared subsequently to the initial five reports offers any evidence for the validity of the hypothesis either, although it assumes it.

In the crude form in which it has come to serve as the bedrock of the Government's community cohesion agenda, there is considerable reason to doubt the validity of the contact hypothesis. The doubts rest on the following two considerations. First, lack of close contact between different groups does not necessarily give rise to poor mutual relations between them, albeit, without their enjoying close contact, the relations between groups can never be anything other than somewhat distant. Second, artificially engineered contact between different groups does not necessarily improve their mutual relations. Consequently, relative social 'distance' between groups is not necessarily a cause for any public concern or a social 'problem' that needs correcting by social engineering. We know this to be so because of the consistently high levels of community cohesion recorded throughout most parts of Britain since measures of it first began to be taken. Many areas in which high levels of community cohesion have been recorded are inhabited by residents between whom there is little close contact.

The official headline measure of the degree of community cohesion within any area is the extent to which residents report that local people are able to get on with those who come from different backgrounds.[2] For purposes of this measurement, a person's local area is defined as wherever is reachable by them on foot within fifteen minutes from their place of residence. Since 2003, levels of community cohesion across England and Wales have been periodically measured by the Citizenship Survey. This is a household survey now conducted quarterly on behalf of the Race, Cohesion and Faiths Unit at the Department of Communities and Local Government (DCLG). In each such survey, the sampled views of just fewer than 10,000 adults in England and Wales are sounded, plus an additional minority boost sample of 5,000 to ensure minority views are not unheeded.

Ever since Citizenship Surveys of community cohesion began, consistently high levels of community cohesion have been found across the country, save for only a relatively few areas. According to a Statistical Release issued by the DCLG covering the period April to June 2007, no fewer than '81 per cent of people in England and Wales agreed that their local area is a place where people from different backgrounds get on well together. The percentage has not changed since 2003.'[3] Many areas in which high levels of cohesion have been found are diverse in terms of the ethnic backgrounds of their residents, as well as characterised by high levels of population turnover. It follows that there must be many areas in England and Wales which enjoy high levels of community cohesion that are populated by diverse groups of residents between whom there is little close contact. Hence, highly diverse communities can enjoy cohesion without their members having close relations with other people from different backgrounds.

That diverse communities can enjoy considerable degrees of cohesion despite their members having little close contact is borne out by the testimony of the residents of many such areas. In 2007, the Joseph Rowntree Foundation published a report about neighbour relations in Tottenham and Liverpool's Moss Side: 'When asked about the limited interaction between people from different ethnic backgrounds in the neighbourhood, respondents by and large did not see this as problematic. Implicit in many respondents' narratives was a lack of concrete imperative for people from different backgrounds to have more contact, and a frequent comment was that different ethnic groups "do get on all right together" even if they have little contact.'[4]

The relevance of these findings to the Government's community cohesion strategy was recently spelled out by Steven Vertovec of the Centre on Migration and Policy and Society (COMPAS) at the University of Oxford. In a 'thinkpiece' published in 2007, he introduced the useful term and concept of 'civic integration'. The concept refers to a certain level of mutual civility and considerateness between strangers from different backgrounds that they must exhibit 'in the inherently fleeting encounters that comprise city life' to qualify for being said to get on.[5] The sorts of everyday practice that he claimed to exemplify civic integration involve mutual acknowledgment and solicitude. They include such forms of behaviour as:

> cooperative motility (how, in their physical movements throughout public places, people choreograph themselves to mutually maintain personal space and avoid collision or conflict); civil inattention (… how people can be mutually present but ritually ignore each other out of politeness); restrained helpfulness (how people enact clearly limited requests and offers for mundane assistance—such as asking the time or directions) and—most importantly—civility towards diversity… [which] probably emerges more from indifference to diversity than from any appreciation of it.[6]

Vertovec contends that the way in which, within their mutual encounters in cities today, strangers can and typically do get on casts doubt upon repeated claims by bodies such as the Commission for Racial Equality and the Commission for Integration and Cohesion about what is needed for community cohesion. These claims have been accepted by the present Government and made the basis of its community cohesion strategy, despite their having no basis in fact. One of these claims is that, in order for the members of Britain's present-day diverse communities to enjoy cohesion, they must have 'sustained encounters' and 'deep and meaningful interactions' with people whose backgrounds are different to their own. In opposition to such claims, Vertovec points out that:

> Desirable as these might be toward promoting better relations, 'sustained encounters' and 'deep and meaningful interactions' are simply not going to occur among most people in British cities today, whether ethnic majority, minority or new immigrant. Apart from a few contexts such as work or school, most urban encounters are fleeting or momentary, although importantly they might be regular (such as greeting or acknowledging neighbours and purchasing goods). Ephemeral interactions comprise the bulk of social relations in libraries, parks and playgrounds, apartment buildings and housing estates, street markets, shops and shopping centres, hospitals and health clinics and other commonplace sites... [W]e would do well to think about how to conceive, appreciate and foster positive relations—if not common senses of belonging— amid the fleeting and superficial kinds of contact that are the daily stuff of urban experience... [A]n appreciation of civil-integration... helps us to accept that a lack of 'deep and meaningful interaction' between communities (defined by country of origin, ethnicity, legal status, etc.) does not necessarily mean poor cohesion...[7]

Vertovec concluded with an observation that some future less manically active administration would do well to invite every bureaucrat and public official to recite daily:

> We cannot and should not expect everyone in a complex society to like each other or develop numerous wide-ranging friendships. But we can urge and expect degrees and modes of civility, based on the most ordinary actions... Daily interaction is what civil-integration is about... Cohesion cannot be manufactured from the top down, or simply stimulated by putting people into the same places... Norms of civility must be enacted in a wide variety of contexts and public places, automatically as it were, and this comes about wholly through experience and practice. [8]

Some two centuries ago Adam Smith drew attention to related social phenomena and their significance. He observed:

> Among well-disposed people, the necessity or conveniency of mutual accommodation very frequently produces a friendship not unlike that which takes place among those born to live in the same family. Colleagues in office [and] partners in trade... frequently feel towards one another as if they were [brothers]... Even the trifling circumstance of living in the same neighbourhood has some effect of the same kind. We respect the face of a man whom we see every day, provided he has never offended us... Neighbours, if they are good sort of people... are naturally disposed to agree... There are certain small good

offices, accordingly, which are universally allowed to be due to a neighbour in preference to any other person who as not such connection.[9]

As mentioned earlier, there is a second fact that calls into question the version of the contact hypothesis that has heavily influenced the present Government's community cohesion strategy. This is that artificially engineered contact between the members of diverse groups does not necessarily improve their mutual relations. In its 2007 report *Our Shared Futures*, the Commission for Integration and Cohesion stated that: 'Meaningful interaction doesn't just happen, it requires a fertile soil of minimal and informal recognition and encounters from which to grow. And the evidence we have seen suggests that "bridging" activities across communities can have a direct and positive impact on cohesion.'[10] An endnote to these sentences provides a reference to a book where presumably the Commission thought it had come across evidence that engineered "bridging" activities always improve the cohesion of diverse societies. The text that is cited in this footnote is some five hundred pages long. The endnote provides no details of where in this book members of the Commission believed they had come across this evidence. Nowhere in the index of that book does the term 'contact hypothesis' figure. Equally absent from it is the name of the person who coined the term, the American social psychologist George Allport. The book in question is Robert Putnam's much acclaimed study of social capital *Bowling Alone*.[11]

There is only one passage in that book that can even remotely be construed as constituting evidence in favour of the contact hypothesis, assuming what it asserts to be true. This passage occurs within the context of a discussion of the impact on race relations in America of the desegregation of its publicly funded schools. The passage in question runs: 'Proponents of bussing believed that only through racially integrated schools could America ever generate sufficient social capital—familiarity, tolerance, solidarity, trust, habits and cooperation and mutual respect—across the racial divide... [They] were probably right...'[12]

What this passage asserts hardly amounts to compelling evidence in favour of the contact hypothesis. However, it could arguably be deemed as constituting some such evidence, *provided what it asserts is true*. The passage in question in fact makes two separate but related assertions. The first assertion is that race relations in America did improve after schools there desegregated. The second is that such improvement would probably not have occurred had black and white schoolchildren there not been made to mix as a result of the desegregation of its schools. While the first of these assertions seems undoubtedly true, the truth of the second is more than open to question.

Since the ending of school segregation in America in 1954, innumerable studies have been conducted there into the effects on relations between blacks and whites of the increased contact that it has brought about. The results of these studies have by no means been entirely consistent. However, what the majority of them have suggested is that any greater contact between black and white schoolchildren that may possibly have resulted from the ending of school segregation has not led to any improvement in the relations between the two races. Writing in 1964 about the effects of desegregation, the author of what is widely regarded as the definitive study of assimilation in America observed:

> In the South... there is no evidence that the existence of separate white and Negro social worlds of primary group [i.e. personal, informal, intimate and usually face to face] contacts and communal associations and institutions has been affected in any significant way by these developments... In the North, fair employment practices laws have begun to lift the 'job ceiling', and Negroes in the large cities are extending the boundaries of their traditionally segregated housing areas and occasionally setting up new pockets of settlement... But, again, in the private worlds of intimate social contact, non-vocational organisational life, and meaningful institutional activity, Negroes and whites generally remain apart. [13]

Some later studies of the effects of school desegregation have suggested that the resulting greater contact between the races may actually have worsened relations between them, rather than improved them. The most detailed and comprehensive review to date of the literature since the 1950s was undertaken by the Canadian political scientist H.D. Forbes for his 1997 book *Ethnic Conflict: Commerce, Culture and the Contact Hypothesis*. [14] A chapter in that book summarises the results of all the empirical studies that had been published until then of the effects of school desegregation on racial attitudes in the US. Forbes concluded by observing that, contrary to expectations at the time, greater contact had not resulted in any significant improvement in inter-racial attitudes:

> The effects of desegregation have not been as positive with respect to racial attitudes as many social scientists were once confident they would be... Children thrown together in desegregated schools, it seemed reasonable to suppose, would naturally form interracial friendships, and these friendships would inoculate them against groundless stereotypes and racist superstitions of their elders... Generally speaking, empirical research since the 1950s has not justified these expectations.[15]

Even a decade later, there is still little evidence that blacks and whites are freely choosing to mix, unless when forced to at school or in the workplace. This is half a century after the end of school segregation. In 2006, a pair of filmmakers who had grown up in Little Rock, Arkansas, spent nearly a year at their former high school making a television documentary. The broadcast was to mark the 50th anniversary of the dramatic end of racial segregation there and how that school became a national symbol of it. While school segregation had been ruled unconstitutional by the US Supreme Court in 1954, it was still being practised in the South three years later with the full connivance of state authorities. In September 1957, President Eisenhower ordered the US Army to enforce the Supreme Court decision upon Little Rock High School after the Arkansas State Governor had ordered the National Guard to block the entry to the school of nine black children who had showed up there for admission on the first day of term. The documentary made there half a century later was intended to show what had transpired during the interim in terms of race relations. What the filmmakers found has been summarised so:

> They found the division [still] exists in and out of class. Most black students arrive by bus, while the wealthier white students drive. They eat separately at lunch and they often play different sports after school. The golf team was all white... Principal Nancy Rousseau said it's an uphill struggle to get the students to mix. 'I push them all the time to get out and find out about other kids and other cultures, and they don't necessarily do that' she said. 'It's a problem that we [have] experienced. I've talked to principals all over the United States and it's... a universal problem.'[16]

The principal of Little Rock High School appears not to have been exaggerating when she claimed the mutual avoidance of black and white schoolchildren was not confined to her school, but was universal in high-schools across the United States. Nor was their mutual avoidance confined just to high schools. The reluctance of blacks and whites in America to mix has been equally as manifest at its universities. Nor has such a reluctance to mix been confined merely to the members of these two groups. Since the 1980s, there has been increased self-segregation on the part of all university students there. As one observer noted in 1994:

> The preference of many ethnic groups to live among themselves is reflected on the nation's college campuses. In the last decade, race-specific dorms, curricula and clubs have become commonplace... 'There's no question that the late eighties have seen an incredible increase in racial segregation on campus', says ... the former editor of *Diversity and Division*, a critical journal of race and culture on college campuses. 'The difference is that it's segregation by choice. Everything from an explosion of black-theme dorms to a decrease in integration within fraternities and sororities. You don't see mixed-race groups eating together at lunch any more.'[17]

This trend in America towards greater self-segregation on the part of its different ethnic groups has not been confined to its schools and universities:

> Americans continue to live in segregated neighbourhoods, even as the poor achieve middle-class status and move into suburban areas, blacks and whites choose to live separately... African-Americans are nearly as segregated residentially as they were in 1954, and a growing number of middle-class blacks are turning their backs on the philosophy of integration, preferring instead to live in predominantly black suburban communities... Today, the black suburbs of Atlanta attract black families specifically because they are predominantly black: Nearly 75,000 African-Americans, many from the North, moved there between 1985 and 1990—a number almost equal to the black migration to the entire South in the early eighties.[18]

What should be made of this apparent preference exhibited by America's different ethnic groups for their own company? The trend has been much remarked on and regretted for some years by several social commentators of various different political stripes. Arthur M. Schlesinger deplored it in his 1991 book *The Disuniting of America*.[19] So too did William J. Bennett, Secretary of State for Education in the Reagan administration, in his 1992 book *The Devaluing of America*.[20] Both authors portrayed the trend as one of the many baneful consequences of multiculturalism. While no less scathing in his condemnation of multiculturalism, the more conservatively minded Robert Bork was less ready to claim that multiculturalism had been responsible for the increased self-segregation of different groups. In his 1997 book *Slouching Towards Gomorrah: Modern Liberalism and American Decline*, Bork observed that: 'Ethnic separatism and hostility to other ethnic groups may be inbred in mankind requiring no explanation peculiar to any particular society... The cult of ethnicity is a universal phenomenon—running from Bosnia to Sri Lanka to Indonesia, and a dozen or so other places.'[21]

Despite not considering multiculturalism responsible for the growing ethnic separation in America, Bork did claim that it had served to weaken a common sense of national identity among its population that had previously served to counteract the innate psychological forces in human beings that he claimed predisposed them to prefer to associate with their own ethnic group. Bork stressed how an earlier emphasis within American schools on fostering in pupils a strong sense of common American identity had fallen victim to multiculturalism. That common sense of national identity had previously served to combat the inherent propensity towards self-segregation:

> The natural centrifugal tendencies of ethnicity were once counteracted by a public school system that stressed indoctrinating immigrants to be Americans. The schools were agents of cultural unification. They taught patriotism and standards derived from European cultures... Now, however, the educational system has become the weapon of choice for modern liberals in their project of dismantling American culture... A curriculum designed to foster understanding of other cultures would study those cultures. Multiculturalism does not... Instead the focus is on groups that, allegedly, have been subjected to oppression by American and Western civilisation... The message is not that all cultures are to be respected but that European culture, which created the dominance of white males, is uniquely evil. Multiculturalism... [is] now, in American education, the dominant culture... Of late, educators have begun to speak of diversity instead of multiculturalism but it is the same thing. University presidents and faculties, secondary and primary school principals and teachers, all chant the diversity mantra.[22]

This claim of Bork's is highly pertinent to how the British Government is making schools change their curriculum and modus operandi so as to strengthen community cohesion. If Bork is right about how deeply rooted and universal is the human preference to associate with those of similar ethnicity, it is quite possible there could well be strict upper limits to how closely different ethnic groups might willingly choose to associate. This would remain so, even were they all taught a curriculum designed to generate in them a strong sense of common national identity, let alone one that was deliberately designed to celebrate their differences. This human preference to associate with those of similar ethnicity might preclude any highly ethnically and religiously diverse society from ever enjoying as much cohesion as ethnically homogeneous ones. Certainly, such a preference seems to be very deeply rooted within human nature and quite ubiquitous. Recent research conducted at Harvard University has revealed that: 'Five-month-old babies will look longer at somebody who spoke to them in their language. Older infants will want to accept a toy from someone who has spoken to them in their language... They prefer to eat foods offered to them by a native speaker compared to a speaker of a foreign language. And older children say they want to be friends with someone who speaks in their native accent.'[23]

Within the conditions of hyper-diversity that mass immigration has brought about in so many of Britain's towns and cities today, the maximum degree of cohesion that might reasonably be expected is that somewhat distant form of mutual accommodation and civility between strangers that Steven Vertovec terms 'civic integration'. It is certainly reasonable to expect mutual civility of all inhabitants of a country such as Britain, no matter how ethnically diverse its population may have become. Indeed it is this *form* of cohesion that Britain in the main excels at. Equally, there are a handful of districts where such mutual civility would represent a decided improvement on the current state of inter-group relations. However, there is no reason to expect that ethnically diverse groups can be brought to attain such a degree of community cohesion where it is lacking, simply by being artificially brought into closer contact.

Not only is mutual civility possible between strangers. The citizens of an ethnically diverse state between whom there is relatively little or no close personal contact are also capable of acquiring a sense of common national identity that generates in them both a sense of loyalty and a mutual solidarity towards each other. In order for citizens of an ethnically diverse state to enjoy such mutual civility and patriotic loyalty, it is not necessary they should enjoy close personal relations with each other. Nor, indeed, is it realistic to expect it. That they need not do so has been emphasised in two recent reports by the Institute for Public Policy Research. The first report, published in 2007 under the title *The Power of Belonging*, noted that 'despite globalisation, national… identities continue to have a strong resonance with people in this and other countries'.[24] It went on to observe that 'shared civic identities have a greater potential reach than measures to promote contact and interaction, which may affect a small number of direct participants'.[25] The second report, published in March 2008 under the title *One London? Change and Cohesion in three London boroughs*, asserts that, although 'contact is alternative to identity as a means of fostering good relations, yet it is inevitably limited in its reach… there are clearly limits to contact's capacity to combat prejudice and engender solidarity. Putting it in economic terms, shared identities offer a resource-efficient approach to solidarity generation.'[26]

Most communities in Britain have been found to enjoy fairly high levels of cohesion, despite their members often coming from a variety of different backgrounds and having comparatively little contact with each other. In the name of promoting greater community cohesion, however, the present Government has demanded local authorities institute whole rafts of measures to ensure that people mix more and get to know each other better. The Government has not explained the need for these initiatives, when, according to its own measure of cohesion, the residents of most areas of the country have been found already to get on well with each other. It is possible that being encouraged or forced to interact still more closely than they already do runs the risk of actually worsening relations between different communities and of reducing their degree of cohesiveness. Why should the members of communities from different backgrounds need to fraternise more closely than they choose to do in the name of cohesion, when their communities already turn out to be enjoying it? Could it not be that the Government is avoiding the more difficult task of focusing on and addressing the very specific social pathologies at work in the relatively few parts of the country where cohesion is lacking?

It so happens, perhaps predictably, that these few districts fall into two main categories. Low levels of cohesion have been found first where large concentrations of South Asian Muslims reside alongside whites, such as happens within the so-called 'M62 corridor', an area that encompasses towns like Leeds and Bradford. According to a report published by the DLCG in February 2008, analysis of the results of the 2005 Citizenship Survey has revealed that 'for the most part, ethnic diversity and cohesion are positively associated'.[27] Only one exception is mentioned: 'Living in an area with White and Pakistani and Bangladeshi populations (but no other significant minority ethnic population) is a negative predictor.'[28] The second set of areas in which low levels of cohesion have been found are those previously unaffected by foreign immigration that have suddenly experienced large influxes of foreign immigrants. A case in point is the area around the Wash, notably Boston in Lincolnshire. According to the 2007 report of the Commission for Integration and Cohesion (CIC), *Our Shared Futures*: 'In areas in the East of England, there have been indications since the disturbances in Boston around the European Cup in 2004 that tensions have arisen as a result of increasingly diverse communities first from Portugal and then from A8 states.'[29] The A8 states are the eight East European countries that joined the European Union in 1997.

Clearly, these two kinds of area are those in which, for a variety of readily identifiable reasons, there is increased risk of friction between different ethnic groups arising from competition for public services, housing and jobs. Elsewhere very high levels of cohesion have been recorded according to official measures of it. These include urban neighbourhoods with high levels of diversity and rates of population-turnover. Hence there are many areas whose residents come from different backgrounds and who are relative strangers to each other, yet which enjoy high levels of cohesion in the limited but crucial sense that their residents believe that people in them get on well with those from different backgrounds. Since these estimates have been taken at face value in all official measures of cohesion, it follows that the Government's own view is that people from different backgrounds are able to and do get on well, even without enjoying close relations. Hence one wonders why all local communities should have been made to undertake special new measures to strengthen their cohesion. The existence of diverse areas that enjoy cohesion shows there is no reason to think that mutual relations between members of diverse groups need always be marred by negative stereotypes and prejudices.

11

School Twinning

Undaunted by lack of any empirical evidence in support of the supposition, positive claims on behalf of school twinning programmes have figured prominently in all official literature since Cantle. In January 2007, for example, the then Education Secretary Alan Johnson announced his Government's acceptance of the key recommendations of the Ajegbo report. Among these was the recommendation that 'schools should be active in "twinning" with other schools of different cultural, social and religious backgrounds so children can meet and work together on various activities'.[1] The DfES asserted:

> The review team found some trailblazing examples of good practice on diversity. Sir Keith's team wants schools across the country to follow the good example of communities in Oldham and Bradford following the 2001 riots. Primary schools forged links by twinning between schools representative of different communities. For example a rural mainly white school linked up with an urban mainly Asian school and they shared experiences through meeting and joint curriculum studies.[2]

In July 2007, the then newly created Department for Children Schools and Families (DCSF) issued guidance to schools on how to promote community cohesion. The guidance claimed that 'all schools can benefit from partnership arrangements to offer their pupils the opportunity to meet and learn from and with other young people from different backgrounds'.[3] In support of the claim, the guidance cited an assertion in the recently published report of the Commission on Integration and Cohesion which stated that: 'Meaningful contact between people from different groups has been shown to break down stereotypes and prejudices'.[4]

In October 2007, the DCSF launched a Schools Linking Programme supported by a new Schools Linking Network website. This website claims that 'successful school linking is a powerful vehicle which enables schools to fulfil the new DCSF guidance on Community Cohesion and enables students of all ages to meet the requirements of the citizenship curriculum and become confident and articulate young learners'.[5] In June 2008, another website claiming to be 'the UK's most up-to-date social housing and public sector news website' stated that: 'the Bradford model of school linking… has proven very successful in promoting community cohesion and [has] led to the Government investing £2 million… to support all schools across the country to set up linking projects'.[6]

All these claims about the effectiveness of school twinning in strengthening community cohesion are open to question, according to the findings of two independent studies of the effects of school-twinning on the attitudes of schoolchildren, both published in 2006. The first study was conducted by a team led by Professor Irene Bruegel of the Families and Social Capital ESRC Research Group at London's South Bank University.[7] Between 2003 and 2005, her team examined the 'patterns of friendship' of some 600 children at a dozen English primary schools that 'varied greatly in ethnic and faith diversity', ten per cent of whom were Muslim. Part of this enquiry involved looking at the effects of one particular twinning between a pair of primary schools only described in the study as situated 'in the North'. One of the twinned schools was a village primary school of mainly white pupils; the other a nearby urban school the majority of whose pupils were South Asian. The second study was a survey of the attitudes of 206 pupils attending 28 primary schools in Bradford conducted during the school year of 2004-5.[8] These schools, along with 33 other primary and 12 secondary schools, were participants that year in the Bradford Schools Linking Programme. The survey of the attitudes of their pupils was undertaken to evaluate the effectiveness of the programme that had been running since 2001, albeit with an initially much smaller number of schools.

Both research studies cast doubt on the ability of schools to improve the attitudes of their pupils towards those from different backgrounds to themselves through being brought into contact by their schools linking. Both studies seem to bear out the conclusion reached by Bruegel's team that: 'However worthy and imaginative, sporadic contact… artificially structured to "address" difference will tend to be distorted by prior group identification amongst potential rivals.'[9]

In the case of pupils of the two twinned primary schools whose attitudes were investigated by Bruegel's research team, little apparent improvement was detected as a result of their having been made to mix. Indeed, some deterioration was detected in the attitudes of their white pupils to those with whom they had been made to mix:

The [white] children referred to the twin school as 'the brown school', 'down there'; they couldn't remember any of the children's names because they were 'difficult to pronounce' and the visits of the children did little if anything to assuage the sense of grievance of the white parents that the outer areas were losing out in funding to 'Banglatown', for example in the closure of the sixth form in the all-white semi-rural secondary school. The children from the white community envied the resources of the inner city school, but treated their days out as external to them and their concerns. The twinning earned the school 'brownie points', but appeared to make only a very superficial difference to attitudes.[10]

Only slightly less discouraging than these research findings were those obtained by the survey conducted in 2004-5 of the attitudes of 200 primary schoolchildren at 28 participant primary schools in the Bradford Schools Linking Programme. This survey did find that, in the course of the year, many friendships had been formed by children with those from other backgrounds to theirs as a result of being brought into contact by those school links: 'All [children surveyed] cited new friendships that have resulted from links during the evaluation year.'[11] However, it is not the main stated purpose of twinning programmes to promote individual friendships between children at participating schools. The main purpose is to improve their attitudes towards all members of the different ethnic or religious groups to which belong the children with whom they have been made to mix. The hope is that any individual friendships formed as a result of being brought together will carry over and generalise into the formation of more positive attitudes towards the different cultural groups to which their link friends belong. So far as that hoped-for outcome is concerned, the results of the 2004-5 survey of attitudes of the pupils at the 28 Bradford primary schools were less encouraging.

The children were twice asked 'how they felt about meeting up with and sharing activities with children, from another school, who are different from them in... cultural, religious or ethnic background',[12] first before they had met or seen their link class; and second after their last meeting with them. On the second occasion it was made clear that what they were being asked about was how they felt about meeting new children from the same background as their link friends, not about meeting those friends again. The attitude changes revealed by the answers were decidedly disappointing. Before meeting those from different backgrounds, 65 per cent of the surveyed children had been 'open and enthusiastic' or else 'quite open' towards doing so. After their last twinned meeting, only 49 per cent were open and enthusiastic or quite open. This was a reduction of 16 per cent in favourable attitudes. Meanwhile, the percentage either 'cautious or anxious' or 'closed, angry or frightened' about meeting such children had doubled from 15 per cent to 30 per cent. [13]

If a country were seeking to improve the attitude of its young towards those from different backgrounds, the findings from these two research projects do not exactly suggest school links are the most promising means. As was stated by the report that evaluated the Bradford linking programme for 2004-5: 'Children's increasing openness towards their contrasting link class... did not transfer well, for many, into a more generalised change in attitude towards other people... from "different" groups.... [T]his jump, from the specific and known to the general and unknown, is particularly difficult for children, who live in the present, and react in relation to real experiences more easily than to abstract concepts.' [14]

It has to be said that 2004-5 was, one hopes, an atypical school-year, containing as it did the 7/7 London suicide-bombings. However, school twinning can to date hardly be said to have given positive indication of having substantially improved the inter-group attitudes of the pupils of the schools that have participated in it, over and above any individual friendships that might have formed as a result. However worthwhile these may be, the stated purpose of such twinning is to engineer macro-improvements in inter-group attitudes. To date, there has been no sign of school twinning having achieved that purpose, and some that it may have worsened attitudes in some cases, notwithstanding any individual friendships formed.

As usual in such matters, more research will be needed to settle the matter. However, there is also need to investigate whether there might not be other, more effective and less disruptive ways than twinning by which improvements can be made in the attitudes of schoolchildren towards those from different backgrounds. Some proven, quite possibly more effective and certainly far less disruptive ways were hinted at earlier in this study (pp. 44-45).

From the disappointing outcome of the school twinning programmes, Bruegel drew the inference that schools should be ethnically mixed from the very earliest possible school-age. In consequence, she argued, the state should withdraw its financial support from faith schools which she claimed simply exacerbated ethnic segregation. It is possible, however, to draw exactly the opposite inference. Bruegel stated that 'young people themselves in the main valued mixing and getting to know others, inhibited generally only by fears of bullying.'[15] Earlier in the present study, bullying was established as being rife within community schools. Would school bullying be brought to an end merely by doing away with voluntary-aided religious primary schools? Can artificially engineered contact ever improve cohesion? The evidence documented below suggests otherwise.

12

Forced Contact Between Communities

Relations between members of a diverse society cannot be improved by artificially engineering closer contact between them, even along with attempts to educate them at the same time. Without sharing the same culture, such engineered contact is only liable to arouse antagonisms between different groups. This is because, however much any specific members from them might develop closer ties with each other as a result of such closer contact, the groups from which they have come are liable to regard those closer ties as threats to their own integrity. Such ties bring with them the risk of defection by their members that no unassimilated minority will want to see happen. Nor will the native majority be likely to feel any happier about its members defecting to join any unassimilated minority group that has settled within its midst. That conflict inevitably arises from the interaction between groups is the central objection H.D. Forbes levels against the contact hypothesis in his seminal study of the subject. He writes:

> Contact seems to be a cause of conflict precisely because it is also a cause of assimilation… [G]enerally speaking, when two ethnic or cultural groups find themselves with economic incentives to cooperate in a division of labour, as they do increasingly in the modern world, they also inescapably find themselves in a conflict of interest regarding the modalities of their cooperation. Who is going to imitate whom? Generally speaking, each group would prefer to be imitated and not to imitate… In fact, one may suppose, the greater [the] cultural differences, the greater the tendency of contact to stimulate conflict.[1]

Given this claim by Forbes, it would appear that there are strict upper limits on just how much contact between diverse groups it is possible for a state to engineer, should some immigrant groups to it not wish to assimilate culturally. Even when everyone has come to share a common culture, how cohesive any ethnically diverse society can become might remain limited. That there are such seeming limits has been strikingly revealed by the most recently published research findings of Robert Putnam. Their significance does not appear to be known to the Government and its advisers.

In September 2007, Putnam published the results of a nation-wide survey that was conducted in the United States in 2000 of over 30,000 Americans resident in over 40 communities of varying different degrees of ethnic diversity. Entitled 'The Social Capital Community Benchmark Survey', the purpose of the survey was to measure the strength of a factor widely recognised as generating community cohesion. This factor is called 'social capital'. Its name was popularised by Putnam, although he was not the inventor of it, through it being the subject of his celebrated book *Bowling Alone*. As he has explained, the expression refers to 'the social networks and the norms of reciprocity and trustworthiness' that arise within communities from these social networks.[2] While not identical, the concepts of social capital and community cohesion are closely related. The more cohesive a community is, the greater its stock of social capital will likely be. Likewise, the less cohesive a community is, the less likely will its members be to trust each other.

Of the two principal findings of Putnam's survey, one was relatively unsurprising, the other far less expected. The relatively unsurprising finding was that ethnically homogeneous communities enjoy far greater social capital than ethnically diverse communities. The less expected finding was that, within ethnically diverse communities, not only were the levels of trust and contact low between groups, they were also low between members of the same ethnicity. In other words, what the survey seemed to reveal was that exposure to diversity has a depressive effect upon the social capital of those who belong to the same ethnic group, as well as upon that of those who belonged to different ethnic groups: 'The more ethnically diverse the people we live around, the less we trust them… In more diverse communities, people trust their neighbours less… Diversity seems to trigger… *anomie* or social isolation. In colloquial language, people living in ethnically diverse settings appear to "hunker down"—that is, to pull in like a turtle.'[3]

This finding casts grave doubt on the contact hypothesis. It also suggests that encouraging or forcing Britain's different ethnic groups to lead less residentially and educationally segregated lives might not be the best way to promote greater cohesion. What Putnam's findings seem to show is that, rather than increase or reduce inter-ethnic antagonism, residential diversity simply produces social atomisation and *anomie*. As he explained:

Diversity does *not* produce 'bad race relations' or ethnically-defined group hostility, our findings suggest. Rather, inhabitants of diverse communities tend to withdraw from collective life, to distrust their neighbours, regardless of the colour of their skin, to withdraw even from close friends, to expect the worst from their community and its leaders, to volunteer less, give less to charity and work on community projects less often, to register to vote less, to agitate for social reform *more*, but have less faith that they can actually make a difference, and to huddle unhappily in front of the television. [4]

According to Putnam, the corrosive effect that diversity has on social capital, and thereby has on community cohesion, is not merely short-lived and only confined to groups that have not previously been exposed to it. Putnam found that diversity had the same corrosive effect on social capital even among people growing up in diverse communities that had never known anything else: 'We initially suspected that the effects of diversity might be greater for older generations raised in a less multicultural era, whereas younger cohorts would be less discombobulated by diversity... Americans raised in the 1970s seem as fully unnerved by diversity as those raised in the 1920s... We have unearthed no convincing evidence of generational differences in reactions to diversity.'[5] Since publishing the results of the survey in 2007, Putnam has elaborated on this point in an interview:

The tendency toward 'hunkering down' in the presence of diversity was true for new and old residents alike, true for both the minority and the majority, for blacks and whites, Asians and Latinos, and in just about the same amounts. So the reason can't be that the 'hunkerers' are those who simply haven't yet learned the right moves in our society... It affected everybody: WASPS and non-WASPS; first generation Russian Jews and their third-generation grandkids who are now doctors and lawyers; the grandchildren of both Italian and Swedish immigrants.[6]

Despite these research findings, Putnam has remained optimistic that, over the long term, residentially diverse communities are capable of generating social capital and of becoming cohesive. His optimism is grounded on his belief that, being a social construct, the conception people have of their own identity is malleable: 'our sense of who we are... identity itself is socially constructed and can be socially de-constructed and re-constructed.'[7] This plasticity of our self-identity, Putnam thinks, makes any corrosive effect that diversity might have in the short to medium term on communities capable of being overcome. He believes members of diverse communities will develop new forms of common identity that allow them to regard themselves and the fellow members of their communities as sufficiently similar to constitute a unitary group:

> My hunch is that at the end we shall see that the challenge [posed by diversity] is best met... by creating a new, more capacious sense of 'we', a reconstruction of diversity that... creates overarching identities that ensure [ethnic] specificities do not trigger the allergic 'hunker down' reaction... The task of becoming comfortable with diversity will not be easy or quick, but it will be speeded up by our collective efforts and in the end worth the effort.[8]

Nowhere does Putnam supply any reason for thinking such an overarching common identity is something that members of a diverse community can acquire any more quickly or equitably other than by their all being expected to embrace its dominant culture. Acquisition of that culture demands that it should be the relative newcomers to it who are expected to do virtually all of the adapting in order to acquire that culture and identity.

So, the bad news is that increased diversity decreases the intimate form of community cohesion that is linked with social capital and is typified by bonds of trust, local volunteering and charitable giving. No one has yet found out how to break this connection, and any solution remains tentative. The good news, however, as was noted in the previous section, is that in most cases this does not matter as much as one would imagine. The more limited form of community cohesion known as 'civic integration', typified by the mutual accommodation that spontaneously arrives when circumstances bring people into regular if fleeting contact, can still flourish, even in diverse communities.

The only pressing problem arises in areas in which such a form of cohesion has broken down or been unable to form, allowing inter-communal violence to flare up. We have discounted lack of contact between communities as a key cause of such failure. Should relations have lately become as strained as they have between some sections of Britain's Muslim community and others, those strained relations cannot be attributed simply to their lack of mutual contact. Given this, facilitating (or forcing) greater contact between Muslims and non-Muslims is unlikely to improve community relations and, in some cases, may prove counter-productive. Something more, or rather something different, is required. There is a surprisingly wide consensus as to what more is needed. Allusion as to what that extra thing is was made by Putnam's proposed solution of an 'overarching identity', presumably a shared one. A common identity is part of the Government's preferred answer too, and it is the solution that the present study proposes. Where views diverge, however, is on what character a common identity must have in order to be able to generate sufficient community cohesion to extinguish the threat of inter-communal animosity. The Government's answer is scrutinised in the next three sections. Thereafter, an alternative solution that has a better track record is presented.

13

Interculturalism—Meet the New Boss

We have seen that both the diagnosis of the absence of cohesion (lack of contact) and the proposed cure (engineered contact) lack supporting evidence. So where does the energy for this direction of policy come from? To find out, we return to the official sources and derive a common pattern. According to the now officially favoured strategy for promoting community cohesion in Britain, recent newcomers to it should neither be expected nor encouraged to assimilate culturally. Rather, all British citizens, both newcomers and hosts, should be made to interact and learn more about each other's cultural backgrounds in ways that privilege the cultures of none. To bind them all, the cultural heritage of none may be privileged.

As with the contact hypothesis, the Government's currently favoured approach towards promoting community cohesion is seldom referred to by its name, despite it having one. That name is *Interculturalism*. This approach towards promoting community cohesion deeply informed the thinking and recommendations of the team led by Sir Keith Ajegbo that the DfES commissioned in 2006 to review the citizenship curriculum in schools. Their subsequent report, *Diversity and Citizenship*, made several recommendations that have since become adopted as official policy. These recommendations included most notably: the addition of an Identity and Diversity strand to the citizenship curriculum; school twinning (already discussed); and the introduction of an annual 'Who do we think we are?' week, designed to enable schoolchildren to learn about and celebrate their diversity. All three recommendations bear the hallmark of intercultural thought.

Part of the three-person team that produced this report was Dr Dina Kiwan, a lecturer on citizenship education at Birkbeck College, London. Dr Kiwan had been a key member of the Crick Advisory Group on immigrants and citizenship education. As she explained about herself: 'As Head of Secretariat of the Advisory Board on Naturalisation and Integration at the Home Office until September 2006, [she] had responsibility for overseeing, advising and contributing to the new edition of the handbook... for new immigrants to the UK [whose] aim

[was] … to promote [their] integration and understanding of British society.'[1]

In written evidence submitted to a House of Commons Select Committee on Citizenship Education in June 2006, Dr Kiwan indicated her strong commitment to interculturalism. She wrote: 'in order to achieve an inclusive model of citizenship, the dominant participative model [should] be coupled with a modified "multicultural" model… [that has] two main components—firstly… "institutional" multiculturalism…; secondly, "Interculturalism"'.[2] By 'institutional multiculturalism', she went on to explain, she meant that in 'multicultural societies … under a framework of common civic values and common legal and political institutions [all people] not only understand and tolerate diversities of identity but … respect and take pride in them'.[3]

Several other witnesses besides Dr Kiwan also submitted evidence to that Select Committee in which they too declared or otherwise indicated their commitment to interculturalism. The Deputy Director of Children's Services of Hampshire County Council revealed that his local authority had already appointed an 'Inspector/Adviser for Intercultural Education'.[4] The Commission for Racial Equality (CRE) stated that in its view: 'citizenship education can have a significant impact in developing… a generic intercultural competence amongst learners…'[5] The Development Education Association: 'The skills and values of intercultural understanding are a key element of good citizenship education.'[6] Dr Hugh Starkey, Reader in Education at London University's Institute of Education: 'If citizenship education focuses on the implications of the diversity of the UK and the need for mutual respect based on a common ethic… it can encourage and promote intercultural dialogue as a means to extending and enhancing democracy.'[7] Regent College, a sixth form college in Leicester, declared its aim was 'to promote global and social awareness, democratic practice and community cohesion through intercultural… education…'[8] Clearly, as an approach to building community cohesion through schooling, interculturalism is an idea whose time many think has arrived. But in what exactly does it consist?

As an approach towards community cohesion, interculturalism steers a successful middle path in the eyes of its supporters between two opposite strategies, equally misguided in their view. One of these strategies is expecting and encouraging immigrant minorities to assimilate, a strategy that, until the mid-1960s, had been the officially preferred one in both the United States and Britain. After that time, this expectation was displaced by the second strategy that supporters of Interculturalism consider to be equally misguided: 'multiculturalism'. As an approach towards building community cohesion, multi-culturalism seeks to bring about the integration of foreign immigrants by not just permitting but actively encouraging and helping them to retain their own cultural traditions and identities. Its takeover as official doctrine can be dated in Britain to a speech in 1966 to the National Committee for Commonwealth Immigrants made by the then Labour Home Secretary, Roy Jenkins. Jenkins deliberately, but very misleadingly, chose to equate immigrant assimilation with a policy whose end was their complete abandonment of their former identities and cultures. This was something that few, if any, of its British or American advocates desired or had sought. In contrast with this caricature of the policy of immigrant assimilation, Jenkins characterised his own preferred multicultural approach as one of 'integration'. This he defined as 'not a flattening process of assimilation but as equal opportunity, accompanied by cultural diversity, in an atmosphere of mutual tolerance'. The rationale for replacing assimilation by multiculturalism as a public policy lay in the belief of advocates of the latter that it was only by according the cultures of immigrant groups such public recognition that it would be possible to win their loyalty and civility.

Interculturalism agrees with multiculturalism that expecting minorities to assimilate accords them insufficient public recognition. Yet, it also agrees with advocates of assimilation in regarding multiculturalism as liable to impede the development within a culturally diverse society of a sufficiently strong overarching sense of common identity needed for social cohesion. Interculturalists rightly claim multiculturalism can too easily become socially divisive by promoting a victim culture in which minorities seek special privileges and grants from the state by claiming to suffer from various forms of adverse discrimination at the hands of the cultural majority.

Interculturalism purports to avoid the alleged shortcomings of both assimilation and multiculturalism. On the one hand, it acknowledges the need for members of diverse communities to share some common cultural identity. On the other hand, its supporters claim that such an identity need only be a relatively shallow one. It need go little further than a universal proficiency in the language of the majority, plus universal acceptance of the values of mutual respect and tolerance, plus an acceptance of the value of diversity itself. Beyond universal proficiency in the majority language and acceptance of these values, there is nothing belonging to the culture of the native majority that interculturalism maintains should be privileged in a society that has become as diverse as Britain has.

So far as education is concerned, present-day British advocates of interculturalism claim that many changes are needed in the curriculum and practice of schools before they can promote cohesion, rather than division. They claim that the school curriculum must cease to privilege the country's national culture and history, and that it needs to give far more coverage of the cultures and histories of other groups. Illustrative of this viewpoint is *Intercultural Education: Ethnographic and Religious Approaches* (2004), written by a Reader in Religions and Education at Warwick University's Institute of Education. In one of the book's appendices purporting to offer practical guidance to teachers, entitled 'Curriculum areas', they are enjoined to: 'Always ask yourself whether a particular strategy or lesson content is just a tokenistic add-on to the curriculum, or whether it is challenging assumptions and frameworks which enshrine some cultural practices and frameworks as "normal" and some as "different"... We need to be aware of imperialist assumptions in the [literary] "classics" and sensitive to parental concerns—for example, many Muslim parents dislike of the inclusion of dogs and pigs in primary school reading material.'[9]

As a distinct approach towards schooling that is intended to improve inter-communal relations within a diverse liberal democracy, the roots of interculturalism may be traced back to America at the time of its entry into World War II. It arose out of concerns shared at that time by a number of progressive educationists at the apparent inconsistency of the United States in fighting Nazism and Japanese imperialism on behalf of democracy, while tolerating domestically 'a widespread attitude towards minority groups... which coincides more with the Nazi-Japanese ideology than with American democratic ideals'.[10] Supporters of interculturalism set up a Bureau for Intercultural Education in New York from which to publish and disseminate classroom manuals among teachers. The last quotation comes from the first such manual.

Like its latter-day counterpart, the original version of interculturalism sought to use the country's maintained schools to promote greater cultural interchange between its various diverse groups. However, the original version of interculturalism differs from its latter-day counterpart in several crucial respects. Its original aim was 'to unite all sub-groups in a common national loyalty'.[11] Furthermore, it was prepared to acknowledge three cultural facts the latter-day version denies. First, notwithstanding significant influences from elsewhere, 'the English language and law, together with derivatives of English values and customs, [must] persist as the foundation stones of... [the] dominant culture pattern'.[12] Second, in the often difficult process of mutual adaptation ethnic groups must undergo when they start to live together in the same society, 'the stronger (not necessarily the larger) usually takes precedence and sets the basic standard'.[13] Third, in 'developing common neighbourhood interests and goals, civic values and loyalties... [minorities must first have] effected adaptations in language, customs and folkways'.[14]

In marked contrast with its original version, that version of interculturalism that has come to influence, if not govern, the present British Government's approach towards promoting community cohesion is one that is unwilling to countenance any form of privileging of the country's historic native culture. In crossing the Atlantic, interculturalism received a decidedly more multicultural inflection. Its appearance in Europe may be traced back at least as far as an international conference of teachers and educationalists held in Holland in November 1982. A summary of the conference proceedings was published the following year by the Commission for Racial Equality under the title 'The Practice of Intercultural Education'. Contained in this document is an account of what intercultural education involves that clearly illustrates the difference between the later European version and the original American version of this approach to promoting better community relations. As the conference organiser Pieter Batelaan explained:

> Through intercultural education, the members of the majority are forced to account for their own culture and to determine their attitude towards other cultures... Education which is aimed at a one-sided adaptation of minorities to

the major culture (assimilation) or which is aimed at the separate development of minority groups [multiculturalism] is by definition hostile to the idea of intercultural education.[15]

At the 1982 conference was an educationalist from London University's Institute of Education who later went on to become one of Britain's most fervent champions of interculturalism. This was Jagdish S. Gundara who is now its UNESCO Professor in Intercultural Studies and Teacher Education and head of its UNESCO Centre for Intercultural Studies. A sign of the changing orientation of his institute was its decision in 1979 to rename its one-time Centre for Multicultural Education the 'International Centre for Intercultural Education'. In 2000, Gundara published a book entitled *Interculturalism, Education and Inclusion* in which he spelt out the new form of education that he argued was needed for a multicultural Britain.[16] Britain's schools, he argued, should cease giving priority to English history and culture and should teach more about the histories and cultures of Britain's other groups:

> Like other European societies, British society has been, and continues to be, historically diverse—diverse in terms of language, religion, territoriality, class and 'race'... The nation state in Britain has... had to mask the pluralism in British society... The notion that... nation states were homogeneous and cohesive rested on falsely constructed imaginations of national identities.[17]

> The apparently solid British core is itself diverse, and contains fragments revealing a Britain that is not 'nationally integrated' but is a plural society... Thus when it is asserted over recent decades, 'our society has become multicultural' (Department of Education and Science, 1977, 1981), the question that needs to be asked is, 'What was it before?'[18]

> A genuinely national curriculum must respect the principle of diversity... [A]n ethnocentric English curriculum does not constitute such... a curriculum [being]... based on fantasising, or on an ideological 'construction of the "others'" past.[19]

> The history curriculum in particular represents a site for questioning local communities and British society.[20]

> Education initiatives which lead to making diversities cohere are important in a period of fragmentation. A curriculum which de-emphasises... narrow ethnicisms can nurture and assist the development of healthily rooted but dynamic common cultures. Students and teachers ought to be enabled to negotiate critically core values to which all can subscribe, and which result from the broader understanding of the commonalities in a socially diverse society...[21]

As well as proposing radical changes to the school curriculum, Gundara also argued for radical structural changes to be made to the country's school system. The changes he proposed included ending all selective grammar schools: 'nostalgia for grammar schools disguise[s] their never having been a significant instrument for working-class social mobility. In practice they... have offered very little to minority communities in terms of either access or outcomes'.[22] Gundara reserved his real ire, however, for faith schools. About them he remarked: 'Separate schools... do not assist in bringing about intercultural understandings. They reinforce misunderstandings... and negate the whole concept of intercultural learning.'[23] Gundara claimed that:

> The demand for Muslim, Christian or other faith schools... only fragments further the comprehensive provision of education... If schools were to become racially segregated, as the introduction of faith schools would in practice virtually entail, the downward spiral of poverty and race would only divide mixed communities or localities further. Differentiated schools can only reinforce divisions within communities. Parents, it is true, obviously have responsibilities towards their children. But the local education authorities and the central government have a responsibility to develop a more cohesive and egalitarian society.[24]

Gundara linked his criticism of separate faith schools with what he argued to be the overly Anglo-centric curriculum of community schools: 'Nation-centred or Eurocentred curricula can only reinforce the sense of exclusion and disadvantage and, in Britain, lead to a demand for separate schools...'[25] In a subsequent lecture at the Institute of Education given in 2003, Gundara went so far as to blame the country's antiquated school system for the riots in Burnely, Bradford and Oldham: 'These riots ought to warn us that integrative public and social policies, including education, are essential if social and educational inequalities are to be reversed...'[26] Gundara spelt out in even starker terms just how far the country's schools needed to go in ceasing to privilege the country's historic culture:

> [A] curriculum centred on the knowledge of dominant groups does not serve the needs of socially diverse polities. In the new era of globalisation, civilisations, nations, regions and localities all need a non-centric curriculum... One of the problems in the implementation of intercultural education is that the languages, histories and cultures of subordinated groups in Europe are not seen as having equal value with those of dominant European nationalities. Such an entitlement to a non-centric or inclusive curriculum is perhaps one of the

greatest challenges to actualising the development of an intercultural education.[27]

Although not explicitly mentioned by name, interculturalism has unquestionably become the officially favoured strategy for promoting community cohesion. Its governing influence can be detected in all Government reports and documents on this issue that have appeared since the 2001 disturbances. Calls for wholesale interculturalist school reform began with Ouseley: 'There is a lack of teaching, learning, knowledge and understanding about different cultures, ethnic groups and religions/faiths. This perpetuates mythology, misunderstandings, ignorance, fear of difference, lack of communication and prevents interaction between communities.'[28] Ouseley also claimed that: 'The continued ignorance about cultural diversity among the school students across all communities must be ended... [I]t deprives young people of social interaction and personal development.'[29] Among the principal recommendations made by Ouseley was a 'leadership and communication programme to convince local people of the benefits to be derived from the district's diverse cultural, ethnic, faith and multi-lingual communities, and to do so through interacting and working together'.[30]

Ritchie echoed the same theme, calling upon the residents of Oldham 'to value and celebrate its diversity'.[31] It claimed that it was 'desirable in principle that as many schools as possible should have a mixed intake so that children growing up can learn one another's customs and cultural backgrounds'.[32] Clarke said the same thing about Burnley: 'The cultural diversity of Burnley needs to be recognised and valued, and more community activities should be multi-cultural events to promote more inclusive behaviour amongst all residents.'[33]

Cantle was no less enthusiastic an advocate of the intercultural strategy. Its authors reported having 'visited a number of schools and found some good examples of how young people from different ethnic backgrounds were able to mix and learn about each other's cultures in a way that celebrated diversity'.[34] The report went on to assert that: 'Breaking down barriers in this way and fostering understanding... will help to promote better community cohesion.'[35]

Cantle was the first report about community cohesion that appeared in wake of the 2001 disturbances explicitly to call for an end to the promotion of anything purporting to be Britain's historic national culture: 'As a nation we have to... accept, and even celebrat[e]... our diversity... [We must] accept that we are never going to turn the clock back to what was perceived to be a dominant or monoculturalist view of nationality.'[36] Cantle did, however, concede the need 'to agree some common elements of "nationhood"'. However, such elements as it was prepared to concede the need for agreement on were remarkably thin and un-historically rooted. It proposed that a sense of common British nationhood might revolve 'around key issues such as language and law, for example, a more visible support for anti-discrimination measures, support for women's rights, a universal acceptance of the English language... and respect for both religious differences and secular views'.[37] Cantle also claimed that 'a meaningful concept of citizenship needs establishing—and championing—which recognises (in educational programmes in particular) the contribution of all cultures to this Nation's development throughout its history.'[38] It claimed that 'a rather Euro-centric curriculum and pervasive Christian worship is still evident (even in schools with few, if any Christians)'.[39]

Several recommendations that Cantle made about schooling have since become official Government policy. One is that 'all schools should be under a duty to promote a respect for, and an understanding of, the cultures in the school and neighbouring areas, through a programme of cross-cultural contact.'[40] Another is that schools should be made to discharge that duty through an expanded citizenship curriculum.[41] A third was that state schools, whose pupils come from different backgrounds, should arrange for them to mix through twinning in ways that 'should embrace both curriculum and non-curriculum areas'.[42]

There was one additional recommendation Cantle made to increase schools' diversity that some state schools have since adopted, but not through government diktat. This was that they should 'consider ways in which they might ensure that their intake is representative of the range of cultures and ethnicity in their local communities'.[43] The Government unsuccessfully tried to impose one of Cantle's recommendations about faith school but was forced to abandon the legislation in face of concerted opposition from some faiths groups, notably Roman Catholics and Jews. This was for all new faith schools to be obliged to set aside 25 per cent of their places for children not of their faith.

Denham reiterated Cantle's assertion that Britain could and should no longer be regarded as a monocultural society. Denham stated: 'Our society is multicultural... There is no single dominant and unchanging culture into which all must assimilate. The public realm is founded in negotiation and debate between competing viewpoints... Citizenship means finding a common place for diverse cultures and beliefs, consistent with our core values.'[44]

In 2005, the Home Office published its strategy to promote community cohesion. By then, interculturalist opposition to any form of privileging of traditional British culture as a potential source of common identity had become an unshakeable part of official policy. The report conceded that, for the sake of community cohesion, Britain's populace needed a 'shared sense of British identity'. Yet it also left it unmistakably clear that, in the Government's view, no attempt should be made to base that identity on any appeal to the country's past:

> Our respect for freedom means that no one set of cultural values should be privileged more than another. With the exception of the values of respect for others and the rule of law, including tolerance and mutual obligations between citizens, which we consider essential elements of Britishness, differences in values and customs need to be resolved through negotiation... We plan to help foster a sense of national and local identity, including through helping people understand and celebrate the range of cultures and heritage which contribute to our communities and cultures.[45]

The Government declared it intended to 'help young people from different backgrounds to learn and socialise together'.[46] It also claimed that: 'Bringing people together is an important part of fostering cohesion.'[47] It announced it was 'committed to help people develop a sense of belonging by celebrating their local and national identities'.[48]

The following year saw the enactment of the Education and Inspections Act. Despite a clause mandating Cantle's faith school quotas having been dropped from the bill during its passage through Parliament, the Act did incorporate many of Cantle's other recommendations. The most notable of these was that of placing all state schools in England and Wales under a duty to promote community cohesion. In July 2007, the newly formed Department for Children, Schools and Families (DCSF) issued schools with non-statutory guidance on how they might discharge this duty. That guidance made approving reference to two still more recent reports which both iterated the Government's favoured interculturalist strategy of encouraging people from different backgrounds to mix and learn about each other. These two reports were the Ajegbo report and that published by the Commission for Integration and Cohesion under the title *Our Shared Futures*.

Ajegbo and the CIC report both were enthusiastic supporters of interculturalism. Within the *Identity and Diversity* strand that Ajegbo proposed should be added to the citizenship curriculum, it recommended there should be provided a 'contextualised understanding that the UK is a "multinational" state', as well as coverage of the topics of 'immigration; Commonwealth and the legacy of Empire; European Union; and extending the franchise (e.g. the legacy of slavery, universal suffrage, equal opportunities legislation)'.[49] Ajegbo also stated that: 'teaching and learning... that addresses issues of ethnicity, culture, language and the multiple identities children inhabit... is education for mutual understanding and respect... This "education for diversity" is fundamental if the UK is to have a cohesive society in the twenty-first century.'[50]

Focused as it was primarily on curriculum issues, Ajegbo was mainly concerned with what schoolchildren should be made to study, rather than with how or with whom. Nevertheless, besides emphasising the need for schoolchildren to be made to learn about each others' different cultural beliefs and values in the interests of greater community cohesion, it also called for the engineering of their greater contact through school twinning programmes. Its third major recommendation was to require schools to incorporate into their annual calendar a 'high profile national event... to give a clear profile to education for diversity and Citizenship education, and... encourage all schools to be involved'.[51] To this end, it proposed all schools should be made to set aside a week during the summer term each year to allow pupils to consider the question: 'Who do we think we are?' It explained that it envisaged 'the main activity of the week being investigations and celebrations by schools of pupils' histories and their community roots and of the national and global links that they can make...' It also recommended that the week 'could include... links established between schools, cultural celebrations, [and] debates around values, identities and diversity'.[52]

The CIC report also recommended an end to the privileging of Britain's historic culture in schools, local communities and the nation. Instead, it proposed that all communities should be encouraged to develop for themselves shared visions of their futures to the development of which every member of them should be invited to make an equal contribution, no matter how recently arrived they might be. In so doing, the CIC report deliberately rejected the idea that the best way to promote community cohesion in Britain was simply to encourage recent foreign immigrants to adopt its indigenous culture: 'Our proposal is… that from now on both local and national identities need to be about shared futures. Wherever we are from, whatever our particular community links, we are all building together something for the future that we can share.'[53]

What the CIC report in effect proposed was that, no matter how mono-cultural any particular local community might still be, whatever form of cohesiveness it might enjoy through shared common values and beliefs, such cohesiveness as it enjoyed was to be made to give way to a new artificial cohesiveness to be created by its members being made to renegotiate a shared vision of its future. The CIC report also recommended that, as from 2008, there should be instituted 'a nationally sponsored "Community Week" with a focus on celebrating all communities and inter-community engagement'.[54] It also recommended linking this week with Ajegbo's proposed 'Who do we think we are?' week.[55]

On the newly imposed duty that had been placed on schools to promote community cohesion, the CIC report stated: 'We see this as one of the most concrete levers in building integration and cohesion across all types of local area.'[56] As well as endorsing school twinning, it also endorsed Ajegbo's proposed curriculum changes: 'Our headline recommendations are: that there should be national school twinning programme with support from the centre; [and] that the recommendations outlined in Sir Keith Ajegbo's report on citizenship education should be taken forward as a matter of urgency by the DfES.'[57] As regards faith schools, the CIS report noted with apparent approval the voluntary decision that some of them had taken 'to teach pupils about other religions as well as their own, and to follow the guidance on the national non-statutory framework for RE'.[58] As well as advocating the participation of these schools in school twinning programmes, the CIC report also recommended 'consideration whether Ofsted inspections should cover RE teaching in faith schools (which is currently exempt)'.[59]

In light of the approving reference it made to Ajegbo and to the CIC report, it was inevitable that, in the guidance that it issued to schools on how they should discharge their new duty to promote cohesion, the DCSF would recommend that they should encourage their pupils to interact with and learn about those from different backgrounds to themselves in ways that did not privilege the cultures of any of them:

> As all children and young people can benefit from meaningful interaction, schools will need to consider how to give their pupils the opportunity to mix with and learn with, from and about those from different backgrounds, for example through links with other schools and community organisations. Through their ethos and curriculum, schools can promote discussion of a common sense of identity and support diversity, showing pupils how different communities can be united by shared values and common experiences.[60]

The guidance went on to suggest one specific way in which schools might go about 'helping children and young people learn to understand others, [and] to value diversity whilst promoting shared values'. This was by their incorporating into their teaching of citizenship the new 'Identity and Diversity' strand of the citizenship curriculum.[61] The guidance also recommended that schools should 'provide reasonable means for children, young people, their friends and families to interact with people from different backgrounds and build positive relations, [through] links with different schools and communities... and opportunities for pupils, families and the wider community to take part in activities and receive services which build positive interaction and achievement for all groups'.[62]

In February 2008, the Government accepted all the central recommendations made by Ajegbo that the CIC had endorsed: 'The Government has accepted the recommendations made in Sir Keith [Ajegbo]'s report and is working with its partners to implement them. In particular, this includes the introduction of the revised secondary curriculum for citizenship including a new identity and diversity strand from September 2008; establishing a new agency to support school linking... and in June 2008 a "Who do we think we are?" week involving all schools in an exploration of identities, diversity and citizenship'.[63] Given how much influence it has come to wield over educational policy, the Ajegbo report is worthy of closer scrutiny.

14

A Closer Look at the Ajegbo Report

It is clear that the Ajegbo report has played a crucial role in shaping the new school curriculum and calendar. Three of its recommendations have been adopted by the Government: first, that schools should be encouraged to forge closer links to promote the greater mixing of their pupils who come from different backgrounds; second, the addition of a new 'Identity and Diversity' strand to the citizenship curriculum as from September 2008; third, that schools should set aside a week of the summer term each year to allow and encourage their pupils to explore the question, 'Who do we think we are?'. Merely to itemise these recommendations is to fail to do justice to the upheaval to the school curriculum and timetable that their implementation will involve. For the devil is in their details.

Apropos schools twinning programmes, Ajegbo stated that: 'We believe that schools need to work with each other across the UK so that both monocultural and multiethnic schools build proper partnerships, electronically and through visits.'[1] Ajegbo further proposed that 'such work between schools must have significant curriculum objectives and be incorporated into courses that pupils are studying. This will help avoid stereotyping and tokenism.'[2] Implementing these proposed twinning programmes, now officially commended to schools, will be no small order. It will increase the workloads of teaching staff and heads, not to mention disrupting timetables. Yet, as was seen earlier, school twinning is unlikely to improve community cohesion and may be counter-productive.

Concerning the new strand of the citizenship curriculum on Identity and Citizenship, there are three respects in which what Ajegbo recommended should be taught within it constitutes a huge departure from all past pedagogic practice. First, Ajegbo makes clear that a primary purpose of the new strand should be to convey to pupils the notion that Britain has *always* been a highly diverse and disunited nation. It was to do this by providing a historically 'contextualised understanding that the UK is a "multinational" state made up of England, Northern Ireland and Wales'.[3]

This approach towards understanding Britain's demographic history and composition proposed by Ajegbo seems almost designed to encourage schoolchildren to look upon the recent scale of foreign immigration as having not effected any radical discontinuity with its past. It seems almost calculated to convey to pupils the message that none of the other social phenomena that Ajegbo also proposes should be covered within the new strand have radically increased Britain's diversity. These other phenomena are: immigration, the legacy of Empire, and the European Union. That this would appear to be the view of its authors is conveyed by their statement that:

> As migration and technological change gather pace, governments—and societies—are faced with the challenge of engaging effectively with increasingly high profile issues regarding immigration, multiculturalism, diversity and difference. Yet the wide picture shows us that it was ever thus: the United Kingdom has historically been a multination state, and as a polyethnic state, the UK's population has for centuries been periodically in a state of flux, with large numbers of different ethnic and religious groups.[4]

However currently fashionable such a claim might be in some circles, it is highly tendentious, both constitutionally and demographically.[5] That the country's schools should now be made to teach it as true requires that they should be called on to purvey what is in fact a highly disputable and deeply contentious view. It also calls on schools to make a radical departure from what they have traditionally taught on these matters. Until only very recently, Britain's schools tended to teach how relatively homogeneous the country's island status had made its populace. Take what the historians G.H. Trevelyan and Arthur Bryant wrote in texts whose like would have been staples in the country's secondary schools until only comparatively recently. Trevelyan asserted: 'The entrance into our island of the races who people it today was completed at the time of the Norman Conquest.'[6] Bryant wrote: 'the invasions which gave [England] so mixed and challenging an ancestry were separated by long periods. This enabled each new influence to be digested... [A]fter the Norman Conquest... the only invaders who settled in Britain thereafter were refugees flying to her shores from persecution: Flemings in the fourteenth and sixteenth centuries, Huguenots in the seventeenth century, Jews in the eighteenth, nineteenth and twentieth centuries.'[7]

Similarly, until quite recently, the standard view taught in schools was of how relatively united as a state England had been since medieval times, and how united Britain had been since as a country since the political union of Scotland and England at the beginning of the eighteenth century. By way of illustration, consider what was written about these matters by the historian A.L. Rowse in a short history of England published in 1943 whose aim, according to its author, was 'to make the story of our people *intelligible*... and to include everything that is really *essential* to the understanding of that story'.[8] For decades after its appeared, the view this book propounded was a quite standard one for British schools to purvey:

> In all the centuries before the Norman Conquest, Britain had been again and again subjugated. After the Conquest, never. For the Normans had transplanted a strong, centralised state to the island.[9]

> The Act of Union... brought into being an economic and political union between England Scotland. Though something of nationhood may have been lost, Scotland began at once to prosper, and not merely economically. The soil of her mind bore fruit more abundantly...: the age of Hume, Adam Smith, Burns, Scott, was the greatest in her intellectual life... There can be no denying that the [1688] Revolution settlement had a great success with the Union: where before was conflict and repression was now release, co-operation, achievement. [10]

Ajegbo, however, seems intent that the country's schools should convey precisely the opposite message. It is one that, arguably, deviates from the truth rather more than does the more traditional message. This eagerness to reverse what schools have taught traditionally is also reflected in Ajegbo's approach to the new fourth strand on Identity and Diversity. In an appendix to the report, it offers three possible approaches towards covering the new strand.[11] The first approach requires schools to focus on whether the United Kingdom can be considered a single state and what 'Britishness' means in a multinational state like the UK. The second approach requires them to focus on immigration to Britain; the third to focus on slavery. For each such approach, Ajegbo identifies a number of issues and questions on which it suggests schools should focus the attention of their pupils. These issues and questions all strongly suggest that the pedagogic purpose of the new strand is to convey to schoolchildren the highly tendentious message that Britain lacks any true demographic or political unity.

In connection with the first suggested approach, Ajegbo suggests students should be made to address three topics: first, 'the chronological context of conflict within the UK'; second, 'how individual nations' historical needs for identity can be, and have been, the cause of conflict'; third, Northern Ireland. In connection with this last-mentioned topic, Ajegbo proposes that a key focus should be 'how religion has divided the nation and the implications of this in contemporary society, particularly in terms of religious diversity in the UK'.[12]

It is, indeed, hard to think what questions and topics could have been better selected had the purpose of the new strand been to undermine in the minds of schoolchildren any notion that Britain had ever enjoyed cohesion. Actually, Ajegbo surpasses itself by suggesting topics like 'What does "Britishness" mean in a multinational state like the UK?'[13] Doubtless, this is an entirely proper question to invite schoolchildren of various ages to consider. However, the specific questions that it suggested in relation to its consideration were well chosen to undermine in the minds of pupils any notion that there is a single British nation to which they and all other inhabitants of Britain belong. One of these questions is 'whether the United Kingdom can continue to be called *United*'.[14] A second question is 'whether they feel part of a *united* kingdom or whether... the UK is made up of four nations not sharing any collective identity'.[15]

In relation to the subject of immigration to Britain and Northern Ireland and the impact that it has had on their diversity, Ajegbo again places a spin on these otherwise perfectly reasonable topics that is clearly designed to leave no room in the minds of pupils for any response other than that of rejoicing at the diversity that immigration has brought to the United Kingdom. This seems to be the intended purpose of its inclusion within the strand, despite Ajegbo stating that 'pupils should be made aware that diversity brings with it economic, social and political discontents and criticism'.[16] Notwithstanding that proviso, Ajegbo stipulates that, should schools choose to cover the new strand by focusing on the topic of immigration, pupils 'should have the opportunity to propose ways to celebrate and embrace diversity'.[17] No reason is given why schools should provide their pupils with such an opportunity. It seems a somewhat biased approach towards its coverage, given the problems that Ajegbo openly acknowledges recent immigration to Britain has brought.

Slavery is another perfectly legitimate topic for consideration by schoolchildren. However, Ajegbo's approach appears almost designed to place native white Britons in the worst possible moral light by comparison with their non-Caucasian compatriots, and without any warrant for so doing. It is suggested that pupils should be made to undertake 'a chronological learning journey' and focus on the question: 'Should the UK pay compensation for the transatlantic slave trade?'[18] Among the other questions it is suggested that schoolchildren should be invited to discuss are the following:

- Why has the British government (Tony Blair) recently expressed 'deep sorrow' for the transatlantic slave trade?

- How did some British citizens come to enslave African citizens?

- How important were British abolitionists in helping to end the transatlantic slave trade [compared to other 'pressure movements'... such as the African slave revolt]? What impact did the transatlantic slave trade have in the UK?

- How and why does slavery exist in our local, national and global communities [in which the UK plays a significant role, such as child labour]?[19]

The approach to slavery recommended by Ajegbo leaves no room for children to learn about how ubiquitous was the practice of slavery at the time England became engaged in slave trafficking. Nor does it allow white schoolchildren the opportunity to take any form of vicarious pride at the vanguard role their countrymen took in ending it.

The approaches that Ajegbo proposes for the coverage of the new strand are especially unfortunate considering that one of Ajegbo's principal findings was that 'some indigenous white pupils' experience of identity issues in the curriculum... [had given them] negative perceptions of UK/English identities'.[20] Had the Ajegbo review team examined this matter more closely, they would have been led to discover how earlier well-intentioned changes in school policy contributed to these negative perceptions. How they had done so has been explained by the sociologist Roger Hewitt. For several years following a series of racist murders in South London in the early 1990s,

Hewitt examined the attitudes of the white working-class youth who had grown up in this part of London. He found that their self-esteem had often been deeply undermined by the doubtless well-meant, but not always well-executed, anti-racist policies of their schools.

Two policies were found to have been especially damaging to their self-esteem in ways that had driven some of them towards racism. One of them was the recording by schools of racist incidents in ways that the white pupils had found neither fair nor even-handed. They claimed their schools had often wrongly logged as a racist incident some inter-ethnic playground altercation in which they had been involved that, so far as they were concerned, had not been racially motivated. They also claimed that their schools were much more prone to classify as a racist incident those altercations which had been started by white pupils than those started by ethnic minority pupils. One Greenwich youth worker said to Hewitt in connection with these white boys: 'Particularly through their school years, where there's been incidents when they've been in trouble or they've had a fight with a black kid or an Asian kid and straightaway it's deemed as a racist attack... and from their point of view it's not always a race issue. It's just been a school or a playground fight. And they carry that with them and... in a sense it's caused racism because they've carried that unfairness with them.'[21]

The other anti-racist policy that the South London schools had adopted that Hewitt found to have damaged the esteem of white schoolchildren related to their culture: 'For some white English pupils, the celebration of cultural variety actually seemed to include all cultures that were not their own. It was not surprising that white children—especially young people from working-class homes— experienced themselves as having an invisible culture, of being even cultureless.'[22] Hewitt relates how bereft of any worthwhile sense of their own identity as white English/British their schools had left many working-class pupils. When invited to celebrate the diverse identities of their pupils, their schools had forbidden the white pupils the use of their own national flag as a symbol of their identity because it had been appropriated by the racist far-right. A new source-based form of history teaching had replaced the earlier narrative English history that would previously have given them a basis for feeling proud of their identity. When, in connection with an event there to celebrate their diverse identities, one local school asked its pupils to name one item in their local vicinity to symbolise their culture, the white pupils could only suggest 'pie and mash'. This rather pathetic culinary suggestion was seemingly made by them in emulation of their ethnic minority counterparts. As Hewitt points out, the white children had made this suggestion despite most of them having grown up on council estates from which Eltham Palace was visible, where Henry VII and Henry VIII had lived and Geoffrey Chaucer had once worked. Also close to their homes, there was an important site of the Peasant's Revolt. Their schools had failed to provide these pupils with the basis for any sense of their English identity. England's schools continue to do so. As one critic of the current national curriculum for history observed:

> There is no longer any requirement at all to teach about any specific personality from the past. Nor is there any requirement to teach about any specific event— other than within a world context for one unit. The defining landmarks of British history are confined to the optional sections of 'examples' of what might be taught... [In] the latest proposals for... a new history curriculum for Key Stage 3... [t]he 'slave trade' is as close as we get to an event.[23]

> Traditional and mainly political British history... courses have now disappeared and the political history of Britain only gets a look in alongside modern social and economic history. GCSE pupils can study such topics as 'Race relations in a multi-cultural society since 1945' or 'The impact of cinema, radio and television since 1918', but landmark events such as the Norman Conquest, the Reformation or the Glorious Revolution have been cast into examination oblivion at GCSE.[24]

Given how Ajegbo suggested schools should cover the new Identity and Diversity strand, it seems unlikely that it will equip white English schoolchildren with the basis for more positive perceptions of their own identity. Indeed, by failing to consider accounts like Hewitt's, the revised Citizenship Curriculum instead may prove highly counter-productive towards fostering community cohesion.

15

Interculturalism Refuted

According to the new officially received view of what is required by a diverse society to enjoy cohesion, it is necessary that its members should all come to 'appreciate and positively value' their different backgrounds. That claim forms an integral part of Interculturalism. It is a view for which historical warrant is lacking. Until comparatively recently, foreign immigrants to both Britain and the United States were received by these two countries without the cultures and traditions of their countries of origin being 'appreciated and positively valued' by their countries of settlement, and often without being appreciated or valued by the immigrants themselves either. Immigrants to both countries were expected to assimilate. In the main, they were happy to do so. While able to retain some elements of the culture of their country of origin, such cultural elements as they retained were celebrated neither by their receiving communities, nor very often by the immigrants themselves. Benjamin Schwartz, national editor of the *Atlantic Monthly*, observed in its May 1995 issue:

> For 200 years Americans have been congratulating themselves on their happy ability to live together... [But] although non-English people... flocked to America in large numbers, they understood that America was characterised by ethnic dominance, not ethnic pluralism... To become an American was to subject oneself to a [powerful Anglo-Protestant] hegemony... [As] a popular guide for immigrant Jews at the time... advised: to become an American... 'forget your past, your customs, and ideals'.

> Thus, long before the United States' founding, and until probably the 1960s, the 'unity' of the American people derived not from their warm welcoming of and accommodation to nationalist, ethnic, and linguistic differences but from the ability and willingness of an Anglo elite to stamp its image on other peoples coming to this country... Whatever freedom from ethnic and nationalist conflict this country has enjoyed... has existed thanks to a cultural and ethnic predominance that would not tolerate conflict or confusion regarding the national identity.[1]

There was a certain amount of hyperbole contained in the suggestion that immigrants to America should entirely cast off their former identities and assimilate completely to their new society. Such a

117

wholesale degree of assimilation was never expected of them, nor often accomplished. This was pointed out by Milton Gordon in his classic study of the subject, *Assimilation in American Life*. Writing of the Jewish experience of immigration to the United States, Gordon observed:

> The acculturation process... has drastically modified American Jewish life in the direction of adaptation to American [Anglo-Protestant] middle-class values, while it has not by any means 'dissolved' the group in the structural sense. Communal life and ethnic self-identification flourish within the borders of [this] group... while at the same time its members and, to a considerable degree, its institutions become increasingly indistinguishable culturally from the personnel of the American core society.[2]

Gordon points out Jewish immigrants to the United States were not exceptional either in retaining many elements of their distinctive identity or in remaining somewhat segregated both residentially and in terms of their primary group affiliations. He observes: 'Structurally and culturally... the "single melting pot" vision of America has been something of an illusion... Culturally, this process of absorbing Anglo-Saxon patterns has moved massively and inexorably... among all ethnic groups. Structurally, however, the outcome has... been somewhat different... The result... structurally speaking is that American society has come to be composed of a number of "pots", or... ethnic sub-societies.'[3]

Gordon wrote of America as it was during the early 1960s. The situation there, however, remains essentially unchanged, as was noted by Samuel Huntington in his 2004 study *Who Are We? America's Great Debate*:

> The assimilation of different groups into American society... has never been complete. Yet historically assimilation, particularly cultural assimilation... has been a great, possibly the greatest American success story... At the heart of this achievement... was an implicit contract... [I]mmigrants would be accepted into American society if they embraced English as the national language, took pride in their American identity, believed in the principles of the American Creed [*viz.* the essential dignity and equality of all men and certain inalienable rights] and lived by the Protestant ethic (to be self-reliant, hardworking, and morally upright).[4]

In respect of what foreign immigrants were expected to do until comparatively recently, and what they were largely content to do, the situation in Britain was essentially no different from what it was in the

United States. Should any more accommodating set of arrangements be claimed to be needed in Britain today for its cohesion to be preserved, then a case needs to be made out for that claim. It cannot simply be assumed as self-evident, since it seems plainly historically false. Lacking any supporting evidence, there seems no reason to suppose policy based on interculturalism likely to promote community cohesion any more effectively.

16

A Better Pathway to Cohesion

The preceding discussion has revealed deep flaws in the present Government's current approach towards promoting community cohesion. There is, however, an altogether different way in which a society that is as diverse as Britain can preserve its cohesion. It is one that has a far better historical track record. Subject to one important proviso, this alternative way of preserving cohesion permits foreign immigrants to retain all elements of their original cultures that they wish to, even if their doing so will considerably restrict their degree of contact and interaction with others. The proviso is that any part of their native cultures that immigrant groups choose to retain should not be so at variance with the cultural values of their country of settlement as to preclude their peaceful co-existence with its other inhabitants or their acquisition of loyalty to it.

This alternative strategy demands and expects more of immigrants than that they should simply live in a law-abiding manner. It also expects and encourages them in time to embrace the political culture of their new home. By 'political culture' is meant the central political institutions and traditions of a society, plus the values, principles and ideals that have become embodied in these institutions and traditions. The desired end-result of such a form of immigrant assimilation is that foreign immigrants, or their children and grandchildren at least, should have come to share with their compatriots a common sense of national identity. By 'a common sense of national identity' is meant a shared sense of the distinction that is conferred upon a people by their living inside the same territorial jurisdiction, being bound by the same laws, by their speaking the same language, and by their sharing a political culture. A people shares a political culture when, whether by birth or naturalisation, they all belong to the same society and are both conversant with and favourably disposed towards its constitutive political institutions, traditions and values. Whenever a country, therefore, expects and encourages foreign immigrants to assimilate by acquiring its language and embracing its political culture, then its native language and political culture *are* being privileged.

On this view, immigrants must not only acquire proficiency in the country's native language, but they must also come to adopt its political culture. That is all that their cultural assimilation demands. Provided that retaining elements of the cultures of their countries of origin does not prevent them from assimilating to that limited extent, there is no reason why foreign immigrants should not be able to retain as much of the culture of their countries of origin as they want, including their religions. In the case of foreign immigrants to Britain, this is something it should be especially easy for them to do, given for how long its political culture has placed a premium on religious tolerance and respect for minorities. The adoption of the language and political culture of their host country is a legitimate *quid pro quo* for their having been allowed to settle and retain much of their culture. All that it demands of them is that they should be as willing to extend to those in their new country the same tolerance and respect as they have been accorded by them. These values and attitudes of tolerance and respect for others culturally different to themselves are not always parts of the cultures of the countries of origin of all foreign immigrants to Britain. Where they are not, their acquisition by immigrants will be part of what their assimilation demands. Acquisition of these attitudes will often be a difficult and not always instantaneous process.

As a policy for preserving social cohesion in the face of mass foreign immigration, the expectation and encouragement of immigrants to assimilate has long been unfashionable in Britain. There are signs, however, of the beginnings of a return to the recognition of the need for it, as enthusiasm for more recently favoured strategies shows signs of waning in some governmental circles in wake of their increasingly apparent ineffectiveness and even counter-productiveness. Until comparatively recently, however, the kind of assimilation outlined above was the one favoured in both the United States and the United Kingdom.

That species of cultural assimilation which it has been argued is legitimate for liberal democracies to make an object of public policy has recently been labelled *patriotic assimilation*. It received this name from John Fonte, director of the Centre for American Common Culture at the Hudson Institute in New York. In 2003, he published an article on its website in which he explained why immigrants needed to undergo this

121

form of assimilation in their countries of settlement. He wrote with America in mind, but what he said has equal application to Britain:

> Patriotic assimilation occurs when a newcomer essentially adopts American civic values and the American heritage as his or her own. It occurs, for example, when their children begin to think of American history as 'our' history, not 'their' history. To give a hypothetical example, imagine an eighth-grade Korean-American female student studying the Constitutional Convention of 1787. Does she think of those events in terms of 'they' or 'we'? Does she envision the creation of the Constitution in Philadelphia as something that 'they' (white males of European descent) were involved in two hundred years before her ancestors came to America, or does she imagine the Constitutional Convention as something 'we' did as part of 'our' history?

> 'We' implies successful patriotic assimilation.[1]

To illustrate this form of assimilation, Pointe provided an example of great relevance to Britain in light of the events of 7/7. The example is of what was said by two immigrants to America at the citizenship ceremony held to mark their acquisition of US citizenship. The ceremony was held in Washington DC shortly after the events of 9/11 and was the first such citizenship ceremony held there since those events. One of the immigrants receiving naturalisation was a Libyan-born Muslim; the other had come to the United States from Argentina. At the ceremony, the first immigrant declared his resolve to 'fight against people who want to destroy the system we have in America'. The second immigrant said that he considered a change of citizenship to be 'a very serious decision' and he declared that he was 'ready to help the country—*my* country' [emphases added by Pointe].[2] Pointe observed: 'The key words ... were *we* and *my*'. In choosing them, he argued, the two men had revealed that 'they clearly understood that in transferring allegiance from their birth nations to the United States, they had assumed a new, common identity with the American people. This identification is the essence of patriotic assimilation and the main reason for the success of our immigration tradition.'[3]

With these two men, Pointe contrasted unfavourably six other American citizens, all of Yemeni extraction, who had recently been arrested in terror-related charges. Five of them had been born in America; the sixth was an immigrant. All had attended American public schools and been described by their school acquaintances as 'typical young people, who played sports [and] had fun'. Pointe

122

observed: 'They apparently had been economically, linguistically and culturally assimilated. This should remind us that economic, linguistic, and cultural assimilation are meaningless without patriotic assimilation, without loyalty to... [their country of domicile].'[4]

In order for immigrants to complete that process of patriotic assimilation, there are clearly many elements of the host culture it is not necessary for them to adopt. Furthermore, no amount of acculturation can ever *guarantee* the loyalty of *any* citizen, whether they are native-born or naturalised. Yet what does seem clear from the example Pointe offered is that more is required of immigrants and their children than merely their learning the native language of their new country and acquiring a passport from it. At a minimum, they must have acquired such understanding of its history and culture as to have gained a regard for it. Otherwise, it will be psychologically impossible for them to develop the identification and attachment needed to generate their loyalty towards their host country.

Acculturation is just as necessary for native-born citizens as for immigrants, but of late an adequate basis for bringing it about in either group has fast been disappearing from the country's maintained schools. That has happened as a result of changes to the school curriculum made by successive British governments. These changes have been implemented either as a result of governments having failed to perceive the need for such a form of acculturation, or else from the belief that social cohesion can be more effectively or equitably generated by the adoption of multicultural, and more lately intercultural, educational policies.

Of late, the British Government has begun to show signs of unease that it may possibly not have done enough, or else may have done the wrong things, to induce such a form of acculturation in its own native-born citizens. One sign of this belated recognition was the decision in October 2007 of Prime Minister Gordon Brown to commission former attorney general Lord Goldsmith to review British citizenship. Part of the remit Lord Goldsmith received was 'to explore the role of citizens... in civic society'. His review was published in March 2008 under the title *Citizenship: Our Common Bond.*[5]

Although his primary brief had been to clarify the legal rights and responsibilities associated with British citizenship, Lord Goldsmith also used the occasion to propose a set of measures to 'help to promote a shared sense of belonging' among Britain's citizens. Among other things, he recommended, the introduction from 2012 of a new annual British public holiday to be modelled on Australia's annual National Day. Its stated purpose was: 'to provide an annual focus for our national narrative'. A second recommended measure was that all young British-born citizens be given the option to take part in an equivalent of the citizenship ceremonies that, since 2002, have been mandatory for all immigrants to Britain upon their gaining British citizenship. Lord Goldsmith suggested these new citizenship ceremonies should be made to serve as a rite of passage that British schoolchildren should undergo to mark their acquisition of the full responsibilities of adult citizenship at the time of their leaving school. One suggestion was met with particular derision in some quarters: that those taking part in such ceremonies should be made to swear an 'Oath of allegiance to the Queen' and make a 'Pledge of Commitment to the UK' similar to the pledges that immigrants make at their citizenship ceremonies.

These proposals are doubtless well meant. However, none seems likely to enhance the sense of belonging of any young British citizen, so long as they continue to leave school as ignorant of Britain's history and constitution as most do today. The present National Curriculum will have spared most of them the need to undertake any close study of either subject, save in that politically correct intercultural form advocated by the Ajegbo report. Such a form of study of Britain's history as it proposed for the new strand of the citizenship curriculum, it has earlier been argued, seems almost calculated to foster in young British citizens a sense of shame and embarrassment, save in the case of those whose ancestral roots lie in the New Commonwealth or in other parts of the developing world.

To generate in today's generation of schoolchildren a sense of belonging of a sort liable to render them willing to make sacrifices on behalf of their compatriots, there is need for them to have undergone a form of acculturation that is no longer widely provided by the country's state schools. It would not be restored simply by requiring all children upon leaving school to attend a ceremony to mark their becoming a full citizen. This is so, even if such a ceremony were supplemented by an annual public holiday to celebrate their country. For most of them will be leaving school without having learned what there was to celebrate about their country. The relevant form of acculturation demands the prolonged study of their country's history and literature. This is something that Britain's state schools have long since ceased to teach.

Without a common knowledge of and interest in their country's history and political culture, there is nothing that can serve to unite and bind the citizens of an otherwise highly diverse society into a cohesive community. It follows that Britain's continued cohesion demands that all citizens need to be made sufficiently conversant with its history and traditions as will lead them to identify with and feel affection for it. For each new generation of its citizens to acquire such conversancy demands that their schools should privilege its history and political culture in terms of what they teach.

Not only must they learn about their country's history, they must do so in ways that are liable to invite and encourage their identification with it.[6] This is a truth that, for the most part, Britain's political elite remains seemingly unwilling to admit. The approach towards the study of Britain's history recommended by Ajegbo for inclusion within the citizenship curriculum seems singularly ill suited for eliciting any such a form of identification with and love of their country.

In recording its acceptance of Sir Keith Ajegbo's recommendation for the inclusion within the citizenship curriculum of the new strand on Identity and Diversity, the House of Commons Select Committee on Citizenship Education stated in its report that: 'We support his proposals that many different aspects of British... history should be used... to engage students in discussing the nature of citizenship and its responsibility in twenty-first century Britain.'[7] However, the Select Committee went on to warn that 'such coverage should... recognise that critical and divergent perspectives... are a central part of what contemporary Britishness is'.[8] In light of its contents as proposed by Ajegbo, one is entitled to wonder just how much scope, if any, the new strand in the citizenship curriculum will offer today's schoolchildren to consider Britain's history from a perspective that sees in its details the story of the creation and diffusion world-wide of liberal democratic political institutions. Having been offered such a perspective on their country's history would warrant and be liable to evoke the gratitude, admiration and allegiance of all its present-day citizens for what it has achieved and made possible, not just for them personally but for all humanity. It is difficult to see how the version of Britain's history favoured by the Ajegbo report will offer schoolchildren such a perspective.

17

Conclusion:
At the Going Down of the Sun

If the general line of argument that has been advanced in this study is correct, in order for Britain to enjoy social cohesion today, given how diverse it has become, there is ultimately only one thing of which its population can be said to stand in need at every level of their communal life, from neighbourhood to nation. What they need is for its foreign immigrants who have come to settle there permanently, and their children, to undergo what has been referred to as their patriotic assimilation. There is equal need for such a form of acculturation in the case of all its native-born citizens too, even though the ancestral roots of many of them in this country might run much deeper. The present Government has rightly been concerned to ensure that there is no repetition of the acts of violent extremism the country suffered on 7 July 2005. Yet owing to its unwillingness to identify the real causes of the tensions that precipitated those and other acts of violence, it has refused to adopt effective policies.

The main threats to social cohesion today emanate from two main sources: first, the radicalisation of disaffected young British-born Muslims; second, tensions between newly arrived immigrants, especially from Eastern Europe and other parts of the developing world, and those British citizens among whom they settle and with whom they compete for public services and jobs. The remedies for these two threats to social cohesion are highly specific. First, the country should be prepared to restrict immigration more severely than of late. One useful way forward here would be for the country not to allow foreign immigrants to enter as spouses before the age of 24. Second, the authorities need to be far more vigilant in respect of the Muslim groups and organisations that it is willing to support and tolerate. This applies especially to organisations that wish to run Muslim schools.

The earlier examination of faith schools has vindicated them against the general charges that have been levelled against all of them. Yet it did not leave them entirely exonerated from giving cause for concern. Some independent Muslim schools in particular were seen as legitimate causes of concern because of the potential divisiveness of the versions of Islam they and their heads were keen to nurture. Likewise Ofsted gave cause for concern, as did the new inspectorate of many independent Muslim schools. For everyone who is concerned to see community cohesion in Britain preserved and strengthened in the coming years, these seem to be areas in which there is urgent need for much greater caution and vigilance on the part of the authorities than they have lately seemed willing to exercise.

The time has arguably now gone when the call for more state-funding for Muslim schools should be resisted by government, if there ever was such a time. On the other hand, the time would appear not yet to have arrived when Britain's Muslim community can be considered to have become so well-integrated into mainstream British society that its schools can be thought to give rise to no more cause for concern than schools of other, more established faith communities. If the arguments advanced earlier in this study are sound, the proliferation of Muslim faith schools might yet prove the most effective way in which to accomplish the greater integration of Britain's Muslims. This would be possible, however, only if the versions of Islam that they sought to nurture in their pupils were genuinely moderate versions of it which, unquestionably, many, if not most, already are. It is the job of government to make sure that all of them are, including all Muslim schools in the independent sector. For the Government to be content with anything less is for it to abdicate its responsibility, not just to Britain's non-Muslim citizens, but to all decent law-abiding Muslim British citizens too.

Many Muslim citizens would perfectly justifiably and under-standably like their children to attend a faith school that met their religious aspirations. They would like them to be able to do so just as easily as can the children of parents belonging to Britain's other faith communities. Not only do the authorities appear to be doing too little to meet the legitimate aspirations of these Muslims, they also seem to be doing not nearly enough to ensure that only appropriately moderate varieties of Muslim school are allowed to operate to accommodate such children. There needs to be far greater resolve on the part of the Government to face up to the task of providing adequately rigorous inspection of all such schools, and to be willing to shut down those found to constitute a genuine threat to cohesion through the

128

divisiveness of what they teach. There also is need for much greater willingness by the authorities to accord voluntary-aided status to moderate Muslim schools. The worst of all worlds is for the Government to do neither of these things. By vacillating, it plays into the hands of those Muslims who wish to propagate among their coreligionists in Britain versions of Islam that are singularly ill-suited for life there or in any other civilised society.

The time for continued pusillanimity on this matter is surely over. Britain's Muslim community is now too much a part of the British nation to deserve to be treated by the state any less or any more favourably than are its other members. They are all equal British citizens and should be treated as such if the country is to be able to resist those forces that would seek to subvert its cohesion in the name of some perverted version of their religion.

Aside from the greater vigilance and resolve that it needs to show in dealing with Muslim schools, the best way in which the Government could help to promote community cohesion in terms of schooling would be for it to abandon many of the educational policies that it has recently adopted supposedly to strengthen it. These misguided educational policies include school twinning and the recent changes to the school curriculum that have served to undermine the primacy formerly accorded to the teaching in schools of Britain's history and culture. These policies need to be abandoned because they are making it more difficult for today's schools to effect in their pupils that form of acculturation that is needed to generate in them a sufficiently strong sense of common national identity and belonging that alone can serve as the basis for cohesion in Britain today, given its present level of diversity.

At first sight, it might seem as if a society as diverse as Britain has become could no longer enjoy any deep level of cohesion, since so many of its citizens now lack any deep ancestral roots within it. However, that appearance is deceptive for two reasons. First, in a political society that once had an empire, its former dealings with its erstwhile colonies will have given rise to shared strands of history. These can provide relative newcomers to Britain who have come from one of its former colonies with a stock of ancestral memories that can serve to unite them with the British people. Study of the British Empire could potentially prove a highly fertile source of common historical memories in the case of today's schoolchildren. It is one that could serve to unite them and to strengthen cohesion, provided it was appropriately taught in schools.

Rather than simply passed over it in an embarrassed silence, or else presenting it as a period of ruthless exploitation and oppression, there is considerable scope for teaching about the British Empire in Britain's schools today in ways that could serve to strengthen social cohesion there rather than undermine it. Clearly, the history of the British Empire provides fertile scope for generating feelings of acrimony as well as of solidarity. However, the potential scope its study has for promoting community cohesion today, if taught correctly, is not to be dismissed lightly. That potential can best be seen by considering what scope for generating solidarity today there is in the study and commemoration in schools of the immense contribution British colonial troops made to Britain's war effort in both world wars of the last century. That contribution forms an important theme in Niall Ferguson's recent study of the British Empire. He notes that:

> Fully a third of the troops Britain raised during the First World War were colonial... In the autumn of 1914, around a third of British forces in France were from India; by the end of the war more than a million Indians had served overseas, almost as many as came from the four white Dominions put together... The Indians were not reluctant conscripts; they were all volunteers, and enthusiastic volunteers... The names of over 60,000 Indian soldiers killed in foreign fields from Palestine to Passendaele are inscribed on the vast arch of the India Gate in New Delhi.

> No one should ever underestimate the role played by the Empire—not just the familiar stalwart fellows from the dominions but the ordinary, loyal Indians, West Indians and Africans too—in defeating the Axis powers [in the Second World War]. Nearly a million Australians served in the forces; over two and half million Indians... In all, more than five million fighting troops were raised by the Empire, almost as many as by the United Kingdom itself. Considering Britain's desperate plight in 1940, it was an even more laudable show of imperial unity than in the First World War. The Empire Day slogan for 1941... 'One King, One Flag, One Fleet, One Empire'... had a certain truth to it.[1]

In teaching today's highly diverse generation of Britain's schoolchildren about the contribution that its former colonial subjects made to its war efforts in the past, as well as by their honouring those who gave up their lives for Britain in these conflicts, there exists a more then ample basis for generating a stock of common historical memories that could serve to unite today's schoolchildren with each other and with their compatriots. It could thereby strengthen community cohesion more effectively than practically everything that is currently being proposed in its name. Such study and commemoration would far more effectively serve that end than would either the introduction of a public holiday to celebrate Britain, that is bound to leave those unable to trace their roots feeling somewhat excluded, or else a 'Who do we think we are?' week, designed to make them all more acutely aware of what divides, rather than unites, them. A correctly nuanced study, and annual commemoration, of all who died fighting on behalf of Britain in two world wars would rightly allow many schoolchildren here today whose families have only recently settled to feel their ancestral communities have contributed to making and keeping it the free country it is today.

In July 2007, an ICM poll was taken for the BBC of 500 young British South Asians that found that only 59 per cent felt that they were British, as compared with 73 per cent of the 253 young white British people who were also polled. How many more of these same young British South Asians might have felt British had they have been taught more than they undoubtedly were at school about the contribution that South Asians made to Britain's war effort, and if that contribution had come to be much better and more widely known and more widely and visibly commemorated? A case in point is the contribution that South Asians made to the Burma campaign which brought about the defeat of Japan and helped thereby to end World War II:

> The Indian Army was the main contingent to the Allied Forces which eventually drove back the Japanese [at the end of the Second World War]... [They formed] the world's largest volunteer army—two and a half million strong. It was an army of Muslims—most of whom went to Pakistan after the war—Hindus and Sikhs. They served together in spite of the mounting religious tensions in India which eventually led to partition. They ignored Mahatma Gandhi when he called on Britain to quit India in the middle of the war... The unique bond between British officers and Indian soldiers was the foundation on which an army... was built that recovered from the surrender of Singapore, endured the retreat through Burma... and went on to inflict the worst defeat Japan had ever suffered on land. In the immaculate cemetery... in Kohima [on the Indian border], there are graves of not just Indian Army soldiers but also British African, and other Commonwealth soldiers, all of whom fought alongside the Indian Army in the Burma campaign.[2]

Britain's former colonies supplied plenty of war heroes whose exploits offer an appropriate stock of common historical memories for generating cohesion. One example is Princess Noor-un-nisa, an Anglo Indian member of the Hyderabad Royal family. She worked as an uncover agent with the French Resistance after having been the first female agent to be parachuted into occupied France. She provided vital information to British Military Intelligence that helped the allied forces prepare for the D-Day landings. She was eventually captured by the Germans and sent to the Dachau concentration camp where she died in 1944. She was posthumously awarded the George Cross, one of only four women to receive one, plus the Croix de Guerre.[3]

More than 10,000 West Indian men and women served with the British Forces in both world wars. The graves of 300 West Indian World War One veterans lie in a cemetery in East Sussex.[4] In the interests of promoting community cohesion in Britain today, might it not be worth teaching about their contribution to Britain's war effort, as well as teaching about the Holocaust and the slave trade?

Suitable annual commemorations of all who fought and died on behalf of Britain would give practically all of its present-day inhabitants an annual ceremony that could truly serve to bind them. Rather than each schoolchild being made to attend a one-off citizenship ceremony upon their leaving school, their annual collective participation in a common nationwide ceremony to commemorate the contribution of all parts of the Empire in its former war efforts would potentially be far more binding and cohesion-building. It would be more akin to Thanksgiving Day in America of which the annual celebration has proved such a binding force.

Participation by Britain's schoolchildren in such an annual commemoration could provide a suitable accompaniment to their being made to learn more about how Empire Day was once celebrated annually by former generations of schoolchildren throughout the British Empire for more than half a century during the first part of the twentieth century until it was re-designated British Commonwealth Day and eventually, from 1966, just Commonwealth Day. By studying how that former half-day school holiday was celebrated, today's schoolchildren would be able to learn how: 'Each Empire Day, millions of schoolchildren from all walks of life across the length and breadth of the British Empire would typically salute the union flag and sing

132

patriotic songs like *Jerusalem* and *God Save the Queen*... [T]he real highlight of the day... [was being] let out of school early in order to take part in the thousands of marches, maypole dances, concerts and parties that celebrated the event.'[5] Should today's schoolchildren be taught about this annual event, in the context of their learning about the British Empire in a balanced light, it might help them to connect by sympathetic identification with past generations of schoolchildren throughout the British Empire who annually took part in such celebrations. That would be another constructive way in which schools today might go about helping to forge community cohesion.

Today's schoolchildren are not the only ones who could potentially benefit by learning about Empire Day. Latter-day apostles of inter-culturalism might especially gain from learning about the Empire Movement of which the aim was, in the words of its founder Lord Meath, 'to promote the systematic training of children in all virtues which conduce to the creation of good citizens: Responsibility, Sympathy, Duty, and Self-Sacrifice'.[6] They would learn that there is a way of fostering a common sense of identity among a highly diverse populace that can serve to unite rather than divide.

Even schoolchildren whose ancestors came to Britain from elsewhere than from its former Empire might discover reason for wanting to participate in these annual commemorations. For from study of the history of Britain and the British Empire, they would learn that, had Britain not resisted the Axis powers in World War II, then not only might Hitler have eventually overrun all of Europe and possibly the Soviet Union too, the way would also have been left open for Japan to have acquired a similarly vast empire in the Far East. Had that occurred, its population would have been liable to have suffered a far worse fate than did that of any part of Asia under British rule. As Niall Ferguson explained:

> The rise of the Japanese empire in Asia during that decade showed that the alternatives to British rule were not necessarily more benign... [I]n its brutality towards conquered peoples Japan's empire went beyond anything the British had ever done... Indians only had to look at the way the Japanese conducted themselves in China, Singapore and Thailand to see how much worse the alternative before them was... In December 1937, the Chinese city of Nanking fell to imperial forces... Between 260,000 and 300,000 non-combatants were killed, up to 80, 000 Chinese women were raped, and, in grotesque scenes of torture, prisoners were hung by their tongues from meat hooks and fed to

ravenous dogs... Even Churchill, staunch imperialist that he was, did not have to think for long before rejecting Hitler's squalid offer to let it [the British Empire] survive alongside a Nazified Europe. In 1940, the [British] Empire had stood alone against the truly evil imperialism of Hitler... In the end, the British sacrificed their Empire to stop the Germans, Japanese and Italians from keeping theirs. Did not that sacrifice alone expunge all the Empire's other sins? [7]

Simply encouraging Britain's citizens to develop a shared vision of their futures, in the manner proposed by the Commission for Integration and Cohesion, cannot be enough to create cohesion among them. They need to be able to look back as well as forward. Besides a common language, there is need for all British schoolchildren to receive an appropriate form of history teaching. For it is only by learning about their country's national history that they can all acquire the relevant stock of shared memories needed to induce in them a sense of common identity and belonging.

History is not the only academic subject whose teaching in the country's schools is critical to the strengthening or weakening of the cohesion of its population. Many of the regional languages that are currently being actively promoted in Britain's schools today are undermining the basis for its inhabitants to share a common sense of national identity. At most, soon there will only be an adequate basis for the development of separate Welsh, Scottish and English identities. Even the possibility that England's population may continue to enjoy a common English identity is increasingly threatened by currently favoured regional and educational policies. In 1992, 17 member states of the Council of Europe signed a Charter of Regional or Minority Languages in which they undertook to revive local and regional languages within their borders. In 2000, the United Kingdom became a signatory too. Since then, English has ceased to be the common medium of instruction in all state schools: 'The UK government now recognises six minority languages for the purposes of the Charter: Welsh, Scottish, Gaelic, Irish Gaelic, Ulster Scots and Cornish. All are being revived, most from near death, and all paid for by the British taxpayer.'[8] The Council of Europe intends that each minority language should become the lingua franca for its appropriate region. 'An official minority language must be used from cradle to grave in every area of public and private life and government funding must be provided.'[9] The areas of life where use of the minority language will become mandatory cover:

'education from pre-school to university, adult courses and teacher training; libraries, museums, archives, theatres, cinemas; judicial proceedings, employment contracts...; place names and family names; recruiting and training of officials and appointing public employees with a knowledge of the language; at least one radio station, TV channel, newspaper...; [and] funds for the media to use the language and train journalists'.[10] The current way in which minority languages are being officially promoted should be a matter of alarm, unless Britons are content to see regional and local identities replace national ones. Why anyone concerned about community cohesion should want to see that happen remains unclear, unless they were hoping that, in due course, some common overarching sense of European identity will replace national ones.

The dependence that the cohesion of a political society has upon its members sharing a sense of common nationality was emphasised in the early decades of the last century by the social psychologist William McDougall. In 1924, McDougall argued that, for most of humankind, their possession of a sense of national identity was the sole psychological means by which it was possible for the level of their moral motivation to be elevated above the narrow horizons of unsocial egoistic preoccupation. He observed:

> Man... can be induced to work... consistently for the good of his fellow-men, and in harmonious cooperation with them, only by participation in the life of an enduring group—a group that has a long history and in which he may take pride and an indefinitely long future on which he may fix his larger hopes. Identification of the individual with such a group is the only way in which the mass of mankind can be brought to live on a plane of altruistic effort and public-spirited endeavour, observing high standards of social conduct such as must be accepted and prevail in any community, if it is to flourish on a high plane, if it is to maintain and develop a culture worthy in any sense to be called civilisation.[11]

Later in that same book, McDougall added:

> Love of one's country, or patriotism, does not necessarily involve or tend to generate chauvinism... [N]ationalism (founded in patriotism) is the greatest of forces capable of elevating the masses of mankind... Man is so constituted that he inevitably develops attachments to those of his fellows who are nearest to him, who most resemble him in their customs, their ways of thinking and feeling; with them he finds himself in sympathy and strongly desires to be in sympathy. He prefers their company to that of men less like himself; he is

prejudiced in their favour as against all other men; he understands their point of view, because he sympathises with them.[12]

The less a country's schools do to encourage the development in their pupils of a healthy non-aggressive form of patriotism, and the more they attempt to promote a vacuous form of global citizenship in its place, the more will they deprive their pupils of the motivational basis for any but egoistic motives. That cannot but be deeply subversive of the future cohesion of their communities.

Another more recent author who has argued that community cohesion in Britain depends upon its immigrants and their descendants acquiring its culture and identity is the former Conservative Member of Parliament Sir Richard Body. In a book published in 2001, Body spelt out what needs to happen in England today to ensure that it remains a cohesive society in face of its present level of diversity. He began with an account of a mugging that he suffered in a railway carriage late one evening whilst returning home from a late-night sitting in the House of Commons. His assailants were three young men of Afro-Caribbean extraction with whom, he relates, he was subsequently able to strike up an affable conversation in which they informed him that they were converts to Islam. Of his three 'Muslim' Afro-Caribbean assailants, Body asked: 'Unemployable and alienated in the land of their birth and now in their early twenties, what would their future life be in the next half century? Unless those three, and a few million others of different racial origins, feel they belong to England and she to them, how can England be at ease with herself?'[13]

In addressing these questions, Body went on to point out that: 'Englishness cannot be a matter of race... [since] the English are a multiracial people.'[14] He also noted, however, that: 'the English are a distinct nation' and that 'someone has not become English unless they are content to accept the core values and beliefs of the country.'[15] He identified those core values and beliefs as follows:

> England is as she is because that is what, for fifteen centuries, the English have made her. In their making she has become different to other homelands; and the essential differences have come about because of a different culture... The intangible feature[s] of [the] country—its laws, ethics and all else that add up to its distinctive way of doing things—more obviously stem from [the] nation's mindset, that particular bundle of values and beliefs special to itself.[16]

> Those Angles and Saxons as well as Jutes who migrated to Southern Britain came to settle and farm not in tribal communities, but as individuals... Their quest for individual freedom naturally begot toleration towards what others said or did. By the time King Alfred united the kingdoms they were ready to embrace a unique conception of the rule of law... at variance with the ways of the Continent and with those of the Celtic peoples. That difference persists and those facts about the origins of the English still lie at the very roots of Englishness, its core values and beliefs.[17]

Body equates a person becoming and being English with him or her coming to accept these liberal values and ideals and associated beliefs:

> No doubt an immigrant's culture may be as good as, perhaps even better than England's. But that is scarcely the point, for any civil society, in the true sense of the word, has to have an accepted ethos to bind its members together... Those who are English because of their domicile of origin ought to have a mindset that broadly accepts those core values, acquiring them by instinct, upbringing, education or, most likely, all the many influences of the civil society in which they live. And those who have come to England acquiring a domicile of choice... ought to acquire a similar mindset. Sadly one uses the words 'ought' and 'should'... because many thousands of pupils have left our schools denied that mindset, and their parents, despite their domicile, have, in the name of political correctness, had barriers placed in the way to acquiring knowledge of how their homeland evolved.[18]

Body relates how successive changes to the school curriculum in recent years have helped to undermine social cohesion in England: 'The story of England was once learnt in every school in the country and schools in other countries count it as a duty to teach their own history. A whole generation, and some say it is two generations, has been denied knowledge about itself... This denial reaches to the universities.'[19] Depriving today's schoolchildren in England of an adequate historical consciousness about their country, Body argues, cannot but be deeply subversive of cohesion. Social cohesion is undermined when those born or recently settled in a country are discouraged or actively prevented from acquiring the beliefs and values constitutive of its culture. Should it still be thought desirable that England remain a cohesive society, there can be no alternative but for all its inhabitants, recently settled foreign immigrants as well as native-born citizens, not merely to be allowed but to be positively encouraged to acquire its culture. As Body explains:

137

Culture... is the bond that binds together a civil society. Removing the bond is like extracting the cement from a wall. Take away its culture and it will disintegrate into being just a mass of nihilistic people... Once a civil society... loses its distinctive values and beliefs, it also loses its social cohesion: in a word it becomes de-civilised.[20]

Immigrants ought to be welcomed if they feel able to accept the culture that has made England what she is. But England ceases to be the land of the English if immigrants want to stay, determined not to shed the core values and beliefs which belong to another country and are radically different from those of the English.[21]

Assuming that what Body claims here is correct, one way in which the country's maintained schools could be made to promote community cohesion would be by once again being able, if not required, to teach a comprehensive narrative national history of which an important part would be the vital contribution made by its former colonials in two world wars. In addition, by encouraging their pupils to pay annual tribute to that contribution through services of commemoration, and by teaching about Empire Day and making Commonwealth Day a high point in the school calendar, the country's schools once again could become agents of community cohesion rather than subversion.

As to ensuring that the country's independent faith schools promote rather than subvert cohesion, there is nothing further that the authorities need do beyond exercising their current powers of inspection and regulation to enforce compliance with all the statutory requirements schools must fulfil to be able lawfully to operate. The greatest obstacle to community cohesion today that the most problematic faith schools pose ultimately arises less from what any of them teach, than from the manifest reluctance of the authorities to hold them to account. For the moment, it is pointless trying to suggest any further changes to their curricula that might be worth imposing in the interests of greater cohesion. It is Ofsted, the agency charged with the task of overseeing school inspection, where change needs to begin. If its house were put in order, the rest should follow naturally.

One obstacle impeding the effectiveness of Ofsted in ensuring the adequate monitoring of what is taught in schools seems to be the continued lack of adequate training, remuneration and career structure of those who actually carry out school inspections. As was explained in a book about the school inspectorate published in 1998:

HMIs do some inspections under Ofsted but this is no longer one of their major functions in schools... [T]he relatively small proportion of the working year in which school inspections [can]... be carried out [means] this cannot be a full-time job for anyone in mid-career... The people who inspect schools are generally casual labourers doing a part-time job, with no career structure and perhaps supplementing their income through consultancy work. Many Ofsted inspectors are former HMIs, teachers or local authority employees who have taken early retirement. Since school inspection is not done full-time... there are few opportunities for these inspectors to gain the educational experience which will enable them to put their inspection findings into a wider context... [Many of]... the 7,500 part-time inspectors have received little more than a week's training.[22]

If Ofsted continues to remain the toothless tiger that it seems to have become in relation to many independent Muslim schools, some of them will remain a grave potential threat to community cohesion no matter what they might be nominally required to teach. It is not faith schools as such that pose a problem for community cohesion today. Rather it is the agencies of the state responsible for their inspection and regulation. As in the case of the country's maintained schools, the solution to so many of the problems currently besetting them lie with changes needed at the centre, not in placing yet more demands on them. As with so much else that is wrong in British life today, the remedy lies in government doing less, but in doing that less much better.

This study began by quoting from a speech given in the Westminster Parliament on citizenship education. The central concern of that speech was the education being received today in Britain's schools by Muslim children of South Asian extraction. It is perhaps only fitting therefore to end this study with a quotation from another speech made in that same Parliament on the subject of how British institutions might assist in the education of South Asians. This speech, however, was made some hundred and seventy two years earlier and delivered before Britain had experienced any mass immigration from the Indian sub-continent but after India had become subject to British imperial rule. The speaker on this earlier occasion was Thomas Macaulay, who gave the speech during a Parliamentary debate on a bill to reform the British administrative system in India and who ended it this way:

No man loves political freedom more than I. But a privilege enjoyed by a few individuals, in the midst of a vast population who do not enjoy it, ought not to be called freedom... We are free, we are civilised, to little purpose, if we grudge to any portion of the human race an equal measure of freedom and civilisation... The destinies of our Indian empire are covered with thick darkness... The sceptre may pass away from us. Unforeseen accidents may derange our most profound schemes of policy. Victory may be inconstant to our arms. But there are triumphs which are followed by no reverse. There is an empire exempt from all natural causes of decay. Those triumphs are pacific triumphs of reason over barbarism; that empire is the imperishable empire of our arts and our morals, our literature and our laws.[23]

To secure that pacific victory, there is much that remains to be done, at home and abroad. It should be the task of this country's schools and of their inspectorate to assist in securing that victory, rather than to impede it. It is a victory on which, it might be said, there depends the fate not just of the Indian sub-continent, as it did in Macaulay's day, but ultimately our own fate and that of our entire ever more inter-dependent and closely connected world.

Appendix

A Response to the Runnymede Trust Report

Right to Divide?
Faith Schools and Community Cohesion

In December 2008, the Runnymede Trust published a report entitled *Right to Divide? Faith Schools and Community Cohesion.*[1] Written by its deputy director Rob Berkeley, with the help of one of the Trust's research assistants Dr Savita Vij, the report examined the extent to which faith schools in England promoted or impeded community cohesion. The conclusions it reached on this subject and the recommendations it made are entirely at variance with those advanced in the present publication. The report, therefore, clearly, merited a response. However, having appeared too late for one to be easily incorporated into the main body of the text, it was decided to provide one separately in the form of this appendix.

The Runnymede report argued that, in their present form, faith schools exert a deeply baneful effect upon community cohesion. Whilst stopping short of calling for their wholesale closure or secularisation, the report argued that radical changes were needed in both the admissions policies and modes of religious education of faith schools in order for them to become agents of cohesion rather than division. Were the changes for which it called implemented, the character of most faith schools would become so radically transfigured as to lose, in the eyes of many of their current supporters, their distinctive merits and *raison d'être*.

So far as the admissions policies of faith schools were concerned, the Runnymede report claimed that, so long as they permitted faith schools, if over-subscribed, to prioritise applicants of notionally the same faith as that of their sponsoring groups, faith schools would remain socially divisive. This was because their current popularity, especially with middle-class parents, would ensure faith schools would perpetuate the segregation of schoolchildren along lines of class as well as faith. Such segregation, it was claimed, could prevent the segregated schoolchildren from acquiring the mutual ties that were needed for the society of which they were part to enjoy cohesion. Accordingly, the first and chief recommendation of the Runnymede report was for 'an end to

141

selection on the basis of faith', arguing that: 'Faith schools should be for the benefit of all in society rather than just some... With state funding comes an obligation to be relevant and open to all citizens.' [2]

The characteristic mode of religious education currently provided by faith schools was claimed to be no less divisive than their admissions policies. The report asserted that there was 'a central tension in the mission of faith schools to preserve and promote particular religious identities and visions, and government's desire for all school to contribute to building shared visions across faith boundaries'.[3] These committed forms of religious education were said to prevent pupils at faith schools from acquiring any shared vision or sense of belonging with those not of their faith. Consequently, it was argued, to promote community cohesion rather than division, faith schools needed to start providing a new and different form of religious education. They needed to stop privileging the faith of their sponsoring groups by seeking to nurture it in their pupils. Instead, they should join with other schools in the maintained sector in providing a common non-committed form of religious education that should consider all the principal world religions currently practised in Britain today with equal non-partisan sympathy. Such a form of religious education, it was argued, could be instituted through the subject being brought within the National Curriculum, since then it would become subject to the same statutory framework as applied in the case of all other mandatory subjects. As a possible model for such a new non-committed form of religious education, the report cited that outlined by the Non-Statutory National Framework for Religious Education drawn up and published by the Qualifications and Curriculum Authority in 2004.[4] Complementing its first recommendation that faith schools admit pupils on an entirely equal basis without regard to their faith, the second main recommendation made by the report was that 'RE should be part of the core national curriculum'.[5]

It was not just to enable their pupils to gain a better appreciation of the country's present level of religious diversity that the Runnymede report argued changes were needed to the current mode of religious education provided by faith schools. It claimed such changes were also needed to enable pupils at faith schools to acquire a better appreciation of diverse lifestyles and sexual orientations. As the law currently stands, faith schools may exceptionally provide forms of sex and relationship education that commend, and in some cases condone, only certain lifestyles and forms of sexual orientation, most notably, heterosexual marriage.[6] All such religiously-informed sex and relationship education was said not only to alienate its recipients from those with less traditional and conventional lifestyles and sexual orientations; it was also claimed that it unjustifiably prioritised the religious identity of its recipients above what the report referred to as being other 'markers of their identity'. Such prioritisation, it claimed, unjustifiably risked creating internal psychological conflicts, if children at faith schools were taught that their religion condemned their acting upon sexual proclivities that they might find within themselves. The Runnymede report asserted: 'People have multiple identities beyond their faith ... [which] need to be the focus of learning in faith schools, and... valued within them... [F]aith schools should, like all schools, redouble their efforts towards valuing and appreciating diversity in terms of gender... and sexual orientation'.[7]

In privileging the religion of their sponsoring groups by seeking to nurture it within their pupils, the Runnymede report also claimed that faith schools violated the right of their pupils 'to have autonomy over their religious beliefs'.[8] As well as recommending that these schools should cease selecting pupils on the basis of their faith and providing them with a committed form of religious education, the Runnymede report also recommended that 'children [at faith schools] should have a greater say in how they are educated' and that 'facets of identities beyond... faith also need to be the focus of learning in faith schools— and valued within them'.[9]

1. The recommendation that faith schools should not select pupils according to their faith

In support of its recommendation that faith schools in receipt of state-funding cease selecting pupils on the basis of their family faiths, the Runnymede report offered two arguments. First, it argued that, if faith schools did give priority to children of nominally the same faith as that of their sponsoring groups, any resultant segregation of children along faith or class lines could not fail but to do damage to the country's cohesion as a community. Second, it claimed that, where they received state-funding, social justice demanded that faith schools should be open to all children on an entirely equal basis, without favour being shown to any specific groups on the basis of their notional faiths. Each of these arguments will now be considered in turn.

The Argument from Community Cohesion

The first argument rests on the tacit assumption that religious segregation in schooling is bound to result in less community cohesion than would otherwise come about were children to attend schools that did not select them according to their religions. This assumption makes an empirical claim for which evidence is required. The Runnymede report supplies no evidence on its behalf, despite claiming to be evidence-based. Instead, all that it is offered in its support is the following argument:

> Faith schools have a mission and obligation to promote a single vision, one that is shared with their sponsoring community. A requirement to develop a shared vision with those of other faiths and those of non-religious belief is therefore an additional and perhaps conflicting agenda...Those faith schools that admit pupils from a range of faith and non-faith backgrounds have greater opportunity to engage in interfaith dialogue from a position of equal status, yet without undermining their initial faith mission. This appears to be the most effective way of enabling faith schools to meet their obligation to promote cohesion.[10]

This argument rests on the assumption that, where children come from different faith backgrounds, the best or possibly only way in which they can be led to acquire a common vision and sense of belonging is by their engaging in inter-faith dialogue with each other. No evidence is offered for such an assumption. Nor indeed is there any adequate empirical or theoretical basis for it.

Members of religiously and ethnically diverse societies are perfectly capable of sharing with each other a common vision and sense of belonging without needing to engage in any closer mutual contact or interaction beyond what they would spontaneously choose for themselves. Such a degree of chosen contact and interaction can stop well short of children who come from different faith backgrounds engaging in inter-faith dialogue, inside school or out of it, however desirable such dialogue might be in principle. There is a more effective way by which members of religiously and ethnically diverse societies can be led to acquire common outlooks and visions besides requiring all their children to be schooled together. This is by encouraging them to develop a common sense of allegiance to the countries of which they are citizens and to the principal constitutive political institutions and traditions of their countries. School curricula can play a part in this. The delivery of such curricula does not require all children to attend common schools. The goal can be attained through a variety of schools including a wide range of faith schools that cater for different faiths.

Within a population as religiously diverse as Britain's, many parents display a marked preference for their children to attend a school at which their faith is nurtured. Where a country contains large numbers of such parents, the prospects for creating a common vision and shared sense of belonging are much better when they can satisfy those educational preferences for their children than when those preferences are systematically frustrated by all children having to attend schools that make no attempt to nurture the faith of their parents. The Runnymede report overlooks the potentially deep divisiveness of a school system that would deprive large numbers of parents in Britain of the opportunity to send their children to schools in which their faith would be nurtured.

The Runnymede report did consider that Britain's current diverse population might be able to find a basis for a common vision and sense of belonging in a shared sense of national identity. However, it rejected such a basis for cohesion on the grounds that minorities would be liable to find the suggestion that they should acquire such an identity as too prejudicial to them. In the course of the report's preparation, it stated some had been consulted who had 'raised their concerns about the community cohesion agenda being synonymous with assimilation and integration into a narrowly defined "Britishness"... defined around the values of a majority faith or ethnicity rather than developed through widespread dialogue'.[11] Such voiced concerns were taken to exclude the feasibility that community cohesion could be achieved through a shared sense of national identity based upon common acceptance of the values of Britain's ethnic and cultural majority. The Runnymede reported asserted: 'Common values were perceived by some as a tool for policing rather than valuing diversity... These comments and concerns... highlight the challenge... where not all parties consider themselves to have equal status.'[12]

Despite the concerns of some of those whose views were sounded in the course of the report's preparation, it remains unclear why the country's population might not be able to develop a common vision and sense of belonging through acquiring a common sense of national identity based upon their acceptance of the moral and political values of its indigenous majority, and a common allegiance to the institutions in which those values have become enshrined in the course of its history. Deriving as they do from the Judeo-Christian tradition, these values and the institutions in which they are enshrined accord to all equality and respect. Consequently, it is not clear why the common acceptance of and allegiance to them could not and should not be made to serve as the basis of such common vision and sense of belonging as are needed among Britain's diverse population for its cohesion as a society. Acceptance of and allegiance to these values and institutions do not demand adherence to the majority faith. The studied indifference that these values and institutions display towards race and religion is one of their distinctive merits, especially for a population as diverse as Britain's. Indeed, it was the very prevalence of these values among its native majority, and the strength of their institutional embodiment there, that made this country such an attractive destination for so many different immigrant groups that have recently taken up domicile in Britain. Acceptance of these values in the secularised form in which they have become embodied in the country's laws and institutions can rightfully be considered a non-negotiable condition of eligibility for enjoyment of the full benefits of British citizenship. Certainly, the country's diverse citizens will never be able to get on well together, or achieve a common vision and sense of belonging, until and unless they learn to accept these values in their present-day secularised form.

Acceptance of these values need not preclude their also being underwritten and reinforced by a variety of different faiths. Indeed, it is open to question whether the general acceptance of these values could very long survive the removal of the underpinning that religious faith provides them with at the level of individual belief amongst the general populace. Not a few have claimed that the general acceptance of liberal democratic values is crucially reliant upon their receiving such a religious underpinning. Among those to have done was the former Conservative minister and statesman Quintin Hogg who, in 1947, declared:

I do not think that there is any hope for... my country unless men can come to regard themselves as members of a common brotherhood. But the brotherhood of man is philosophically meaningless and practically unattainable except in the light of the universal Fatherhood of God... Neither of the two great commandments can be practised separately, for the love of God does not exist in the man who does not love his brother whom he has seen, and the love of man is impossible, or at least foolish, except in the grace and understanding bestowed by faith in, and love of, God.[13]

If what Hogg claims here is correct, then not only would it be folly for any of Britain's present-day ethnic or religious minorities to suppose they had any just cause to reject the values of its ethnic and religious majority in their contemporary secularised form. It would equally be folly for them or anyone else to think that Britain stood much of a chance of being able to enjoy any appreciable degree of community cohesion in future unless religious faith continued to be nurtured within its schools in such forms as were consonant with those values.

The need for the sake of community cohesion for schools to nurture religious faith is especially pressing given the tenuous hold of organised forms of religion upon the general populace in Britain today. In such circumstances, far from threatening community cohesion, the provision by its faith schools of suitably moderate faith-nurturing forms of religious education would be a vital condition of any such country enjoying much cohesion. In so far as faith schools admit pupils without regard to their faith, it becomes more difficult for them to provide such committed forms of religious education.

Not only are there theoretical considerations that suggest that faith schools with exclusive admissions policies need not be prejudicial to community cohesion, there are empirical considerations which suggest this too. A considerable body of published research exists that shows pupils at religiously segregated faith schools can be every bit as able as any other children to acquire a common vision and shared sense of belonging with those not of their faith. In the early 1990s, a survey was conducted in Northern Ireland of 2,000 children attending 19 secondary schools of which ten were Protestant and nine were Roman Catholic. It found that: 'Throughout the age range and for both sexes and both denominational groups there was a positive relationship between attitude towards religion and openness. The young people most favourably disposed towards religion were also most open to members of the other religious groups.'[14] In the latter part of 2000 and early part of 2001, a similar but smaller-scale study was conducted of the attitudes and out-of-school behaviour of pupils attending a number of exclusively Jewish schools in north-west London. Many of the children whose attitudes and behaviour were investigated had attended no other sorts of school. It was found that: 'almost all of them emphatically rejected the argument that attending a Jewish school makes mixing with non-Jews problematic.'[15] Many reported themselves as having many close friends who were not of their faith and with whom they regularly fraternised outside of school. The Runnymede report made no reference at all to any of this published research. It is hard to believe those responsible for the report could have been unaware of it, since the research is both well-known and is often referred to in the relevant literature. Omission of any reference to it is most surprising, to say the least, in a report that prides itself on having been 'evidence-based'.[16]

Despite such empirical research as suggests that faith schools operating with exclusive admissions policies need not necessarily impede community cohesion, some might still wish to claim that these schools could make an even better job of promoting community cohesion were those selective admissions policies scrapped in favour of open admissions. Certainly, were faith schools to become religiously mixed, their pupils would be accorded better opportunity to engage during school hours in inter-faith dialogue with children of other faiths. Whether their being accorded such opportunities would necessarily improve inter-communal relations between children of different back-grounds, however, is open to question. Britain's community schools do not select pupils on the basis of faith. Moreover, when religiously mixed, these schools increasingly teach religious education in a way designed to encourage their pupils to engage in dialogue with those not of their faith.[17] However, the incidence of bullying and violence in schools in Britain is the highest in Europe.[18] Moreover, such bullying and violence increasingly takes place because of racial or religious differences between victims and their assailants.[19] Given these unpleasant facts, there seems little basis for confidence that, were faith schools to open their admissions to all children on an equal basis regardless of their faiths, such schools would necessarily lead their pupils to share with those not of their faith any greater sense of belonging and vision than they currently do. The track-record of the country's community schools does not exactly inspire confidence on this score.

The argument from fairness

As well as claiming that community cohesion would be enhanced if faith schools were to admit pupils on an entirely equal basis regardless of their faiths, the Runnymede report also argued that faith schools in receipt of public money are under a moral obligation to do so. It declared: 'With state funding comes an obligation to be... open to all citizens'.[20]

A moment's reflection should suffice to lay bare a fatal flaw with this argument. Considerations of equity and social justice only demand that like cases should be treated similarly. Whether children from different faith backgrounds are sufficiently alike so as to qualify equally to attend schools that have been established to nurture the faiths of only some of them is open to question. Their equal entitlement to attend such schools is especially questionable, when the extra costs of providing for the nurturance of faith by those schools has been wholly borne by a group that adheres to it and that might well have been unwilling to bear them save for that express purpose.

It is true that children who come from different faith backgrounds all stand equally in need of and are equally entitled to state-schooling. It might also be true of all children that they stand to benefit from attending faith schools established to nurture the faiths of only some of them. Such facts do not establish the equal entitlement of all children to attend all faith schools that receive public funding any more than the fact that a man and a woman might both, on some occasion, stand equally to benefit from using a public convenience, intended for only one of the sexes, establishes their equal entitlement to its use.

Were the general principle valid to which the Runnymede report appeals in support of its contention that faith schools which receive public funding have an obligation to be open to all on an equal basis, the state would no longer be entitled to provide separate-sex public conveniences and NHS hospital wards. Furthermore, all maintained schools would have to open their admissions on an equal basis to all British citizens, irrespective of their age. Although there might well be some who think that all publicly-funded schools should be open to all

British citizens on an equal basis, mercifully their number is small and for very good reason. Clearly, that to which publicly-funded facilities should provide everyone with equal access is that range of benefits that these facilities collectively provide, but which each facility might well have good reason to reserve for the use of only some of them. In the case of hospital wards and public conveniences, there is no reason why each of these amenities should be open to both sexes on an equal basis, provided the two sexes enjoy equal access to equivalent amenities on the basis of equal need. To open up each and every publicly-funded facility to both sexes on an equal basis would arguably do neither sex any favours.

Some might be willing to concede the equity of separate-sex public amenities such as hospital wards and public conveniences, but deny the fairness of publicly-funded faith schools when they operate with selective admissions policies that favour the children of one faith above others. Despite receiving no more from the state per child than community schools, faith schools consistently outperform community schools in examinations.[21] With better examination results generally follow better life-chances for their pupils. The supporters of faith schools attribute their generally better examination results to the religious ethos of these schools which in turn they in part attribute to their selective admissions policies, since they make their nurturance of the faith of their sponsoring groups much easier. Opponents of religious selective faith schools are more inclined to attribute their generally better examination results to their pupils allegedly coming from more settled or affluent families by which they are rendered more easily educible. Through being concentrated in faith schools, these more easily educible children derive the extra benefit of their co-schooling. Meanwhile, the benefits of being schooled alongside more educible peers are denied to children from less affluent or settled backgrounds, who, because of their ineligibility to attend over-subscribed faith schools or lack of parental concern or nous to place them at one, tend to end up through no fault of their own at less well-achieving community schools.

The claim that the generally better examination results of faith schools is due to their more largely middle-class intakes has become far less credible since the publication, shortly after the Runnymede report, of analyses of the assessment results of pupils at England's maintained schools in the school-year ending July 2007. As well as consistently outperforming community schools at all key-stage levels of assessment, faith schools were also found to outperform community schools even by the measure of their 'value-added'. This measure involves weighting the examination results of schools to discount any educational advantage their pupils might gain by having come from more affluent homes:

> The 'value-added' measure... compares performance at 16 to results when pupils started at 11. Scores are weighted to take account of the number of pupils speaking English as a second language and those on free meals—ensuring schools with large numbers of middle-class children do not gain unfair advantage. On this measure, Muslim pupils [at Muslim faith schools] made the most progress, followed by those at Jewish schools, 'other' Christian schools, Catholic schools and Anglican schools. Again they [all] outstripped secular schools. It suggests that claims faith schools are dominated by children from rich backgrounds may be exaggerated.[22]

Whether the greater success in examinations of faith schools is owed more to their religious ethos than to their indirect selection of more educible children is liable to remain a moot subject for a long time. However, sometimes it seems that some opponents of selective faith schools would prefer all faith schools to perform as poorly as the average community school rather than any should achieve better than average examination results. It is certainly open to question whether they would be able to preserve their current comparatively high academic standards, let alone their distinct religious ethos, were they to open up their admissions to children of all faiths on a strictly equal basis. So too is the question whether faith schools that do select on a faith basis are, in practice, any more selective of more easily educible middle-class children than are 'non-selective' community schools situated in exclusively or predominantly middle-class catchments areas.

Doubtless, some educational zealots will not rest content until all state schools have been made exactly alike in terms of the social backgrounds of their pupils. Short of abolishing the family, private property and a market economy, however, their prospects for success in this matter seem nil. That being so, and post-code selection seemingly being morally no better than selection according to the faith of pupils, the best remedy to the problem of a shortage of places at high-achieving faith schools would seem to be for the state to open more of them in response to parental demand.

We have now concluded our examination of the considerations adduced by the Runnymede Report on behalf of its recommendation that faith schools should open their admissions to all children on an equal basis regardless of their faiths. These considerations have been found not to provide an adequate basis for that recommendation. Indeed, we found some reason to think that community cohesion would be better served by faith schools not implementing it.

We now turn to the considerations that the Runnymede report adduced on behalf of its recommendation that, for the sake of stronger community cohesion as well as the rights of their pupils, faith schools should cease to provide religious education in a form designed to nurture the faith of their sponsoring group in their pupils. Instead, so the recommendation runs, such schools should join with other state schools in teaching their pupils about all faiths, lifestyles and sexual orientations that are present in Britain today without favouring any of them.

2. The recommendation that faith schools should not privilege their faith in what they teach

The Runnymede report offered two considerations on behalf of its recommendation that faith schools should discard their traditionally committed modes of religious education in favour of one that sought not to nurture any, but rather taught about all the main faiths practised in Britain today without favouring any of them. The first consideration was the need that the report claimed children growing up in Britain today have to become better informed about the various faiths, lifestyles and sexual orientations present among its population. This need was posited on the grounds that their better information about these matters would facilitate better relations between those possessed of these different faiths, lifestyles and sexual orientations. The second consideration was the alleged right that the report posited children had to decide for themselves what faith, lifestyle and sexual orientation to adopt.

The argument from diversity

As regards the first consideration, two points may be made in defence of faith schools retaining their traditionally committed modes of religious education. First, however desirable it might be that children growing up today in Britain should learn about the different religions now practised there, the time available in school for them to do so is strictly limited. In the past, the reason why religious education was a compulsory subject had nothing to do with the supposed desirability of schoolchildren learning about all the main world religions or even about all those practised in Britain. It was made compulsory for schoolchildren, unless their parents withdrew them on conscientious grounds from such study and assemblies, because the nurturance by schools in their pupils of the presumed faith of their parents was judged essential to their spiritual development. Such a belief is no longer so widely shared, especially among the country's political and educational elite. This, however, is not an adequate reason why religious education should remain a compulsory school subject but turned into the non-confessional study of all major world religions practised in Britain. It is, rather, a reason why religious education should cease to be a compulsory school subject, save in faith schools that are founded and remain partly funded by faith groups so as to nurture children in the faith of their parents.

The real issue, therefore, is not so much whether such religious education as faith schools provide be committed and faith-nurturing or the neutral study of all the main religions practised in Britain. Rather, it is whether state-funded community schools should oblige their pupils to learn about religion throughout the period of their compulsory schooling in a way not intended to nurture any form of faith in them. There is no particular reason to think the non-committed study of religion by all schoolchildren should be considered so desirable as to justify their being required to study religion throughout their compulsory schooling. There are, however, several very good reasons why even community schools should retain religious education as a compulsory subject in a form that does seek to nurture in their pupils whatever is the faith of their parents. One such reason is that, in an age such as the present when participation in organised religious observance has fallen away among very large swathes of the general population, receipt in school of some committed form of religious education is often the only exposure children have to any systematic attempt at its nurturance. Despite the majority of the populace no longer being particularly devout or observant, most of them still continue to remain religiously self-identified.[23] It can therefore safely be presumed that most would want their children brought up in the same faith as theirs wherever possible. Such a presumed parental preference is, therefore, one very good reason why even community schools should continue to provide a committed form of religious education wherever it can be provided without parental objection.

A second reason why all schools in Britain should ideally continue to provide religious education in a committed form was earlier hinted at in the quotation from Quintin Hogg. More recently, this reason was spelt out still more clearly in a defence of religious education offered by the Scottish philosopher John Haldane. He observed:

> In this country as in the West generally (and beyond it) the culture is predominantly that of Judaeo-Christianity. Moreover, this is not simply a fact about its historical origins... [T]he values presupposed in social life (and, derivatively, in 'individual' life also) have their source in this religious tradition. Moreover, they continue to derive sustenance from it... The notions of freedom, moral equality and social responsibility... themselves derive both meaning and justification from... Christian doctrines... [as does] the thought that... there is some respect in which all are equal and hence require equable treatment.[24]

Doubtless, similar moral intuitions are capable of being found at the root of most versions of the other world-religions currently practised in Britain, especially those within the so-called same Abrahamic tradition as Christianity. However, it still remains the case that the vast majority of Britain's population are self-identifying Christians.[25] Should Quintin Hogg and John Haldane be correct in what they assert about the dependency of the general acceptance of liberal values upon religious commitments, then for the Runnymede Trust to recommend state schools not provide any committed form of religious education is tantamount to its recommending that the branch on which Britain's religious and ethnic minorities have been able to perch comfortably for many past decades now be sawn off. Certainly, it may be argued that children growing up in Britain today would derive so much benefit from learning about all the main world-religions currently practised there as to justify inclusion of their study as a compulsory part of their school curriculum. Even so, there is no reason to think such study could not adequately be provided without need of any schools, let alone faith schools, having to make room for it by abandoning committed faith-nurturing modes of religious education.

Not only is there no good reason why faith schools should institute such wholesale changes in their traditionally committed modes of religious education as the Runnymede report recommended they should. There is good reason to think that such study of other religions besides whichever may be nurtured in children at home and school is best postponed until after they have undergone a long period of schooling during which it is only to the study of their own faith to which they have been exposed at school.[26] Many supporters of faith schools have long been at pains to point out the educational damage to the religious formation of children incurred by their too early exposure to the study of religions other than that of their own families. This potential damage has been a continued major objection to the sort of non-confessional, multi-faith religious education whose introduction into all state schools the Runnymede report would recommend.

One variant of this objection was given by David Hargreaves, a former chief inspector of the Inner London Education Authority and a former professor of education at Cambridge University. In a pamphlet published in 1994 by the think-tank Demos under the title *The Mosaic of Learning: Schools and Teachers for the Next Century*, Hargreaves observed: 'The notion of a non-denominational core RE to be offered in all schools... is becoming less and less viable and should now be abandoned. The multi-faith pick 'n' mix tour of religions easily trivialises each faith's claims to truth. As an academic discipline, it has little appeal to most children and comes before they are mature enough to engage in the necessary historical and philosophical analysis.'[27] In this pamphlet, Hargreaves intimated that he would sooner see religious education removed as a compulsory subject from community schools than introduced into faith schools as the non-committed study of world-religions which the Runnymede would seek to foist on all of them. Perhaps, it would be still better were humanists and atheists able to sponsor schools open to all children and from which all committed forms of religious education were entirely absent, and to see how well such schools fared in competition with other sorts of schools.

The form of religious education that the Runnymede report recommended should be introduced into all maintained schools is not only liable to confuse children, if offered too early. It is also liable to militate against the religious formation of those children whose parents are not especially devout or observant but who nonetheless wish their children to receive a committed form of religious education at school. As Simon Pearce observed in 1986 in a response to the similar multi-faith nostrums contained in the 1985 Swann Report, *Education for All*:

> Many... pupils, whose parents are not churchgoers... wish their children to receive a grounding in Christianity... [They] will certainly lose out on a syllabus which allows it to compete for the scanty time allocated to RE with other religions... But there is another, deeper, objection to the multi-faith syllabus... An RE which is based on cultural pluralism, which demands that all faiths be presented as 'valid belief systems in their own right', is likely to fudge... basic questions and, by majoring on ethics, convey the impression that spiritual matters are less important. There will be an inevitable temptation to imply that, at bottom, all faiths are the same.[28]

That all faiths are, at bottom, the same is an impression that those who take some faith very seriously seldom want their children to acquire. They typically would like to see their children coming to adhere to the same faith as they do. The form of religious education that the Runnymede report recommends for faith schools would militate against that outcome. Its recommendation that religious education in state schools become merely the non-committed study of all the main world religions would also seem equally unsuited to meeting the wishes of not-particularly devout parents who nonetheless still identify with some religion and wish their children to be brought up in that faith. This point was made by Rowan Williams in the first address he gave after becoming Archbishop of Canterbury in 2003. He remarked:

> The fact is that very many students in a church school will have their primary exposure to shared religious activity in school. They and their families will not regularly and invariably be part of a worshipping group, whatever motions may have been gone through by parents to win places. What the school does corporately as a Christian body will be, to all intent and purposes, how these parents and students will experience the reality of the Church.[29]

In such circumstances, for the Runnymede report to call upon church schools to abandon their committed form of religious education seems to border upon wanting to see the Church of England commit *hara-kiri*. What holds true of the Anglican Church holds no less true of the many other faiths in Britain for the nurturance of which faith schools have been, and are currently in process of being, established. The recommendations of the Runnymede report would appear not only to be imperilling the safety and security of minorities by possibly removing the religious basis for the tolerance and respect they are shown by the majority. It would also seem to be imperilling the ability of religious minorities to preserve their faiths.

The argument from the need to respect unconventional lifestyles

'But what about the rights of those children to decide on these matters themselves? Moreover, what about the need to ensure all children become suitably acquainted in school with Britain's current diversity of faith, lifestyle and sexual orientation in ways that lead them to appreciate and value them all?' With these questions, we return to the second consideration adduced by the Runnymede report on behalf of its recommendation that faith schools should jettison their currently committed form of religious education for a non-committed form of such education that merely teaches children about all faiths present in Britain today without seeking to nurture in them any one or any particular lifestyle or sexual orientation. The Runnymede report claimed that only such an entirely non-committed form of religious education can sustain community cohesion in a society so diverse as Britain has become and adequately respect children's rights to autonomy.

It is indeed paradoxical that the Runnymede report should call for what would in practice amount to much greater educational uniformity on the part of faith schools for the supposed sake of thereby leading their pupils better to appreciate and value religious and cultural diversity. As John Haldane explains:

> It is not a mark of respect for Catholicism to delight in dainty crucifixes around children's necks but to frown upon the placing of a wooden cross above the classroom in which they sit, or upon the saying of prayers before lessons begin. Similarly one does no justice to non-Christian faiths by encouraging certain of their associated customs and practices as part of a 'celebration of cultural diversity', while simultaneously discouraging the establishment of schools committed to the transmission of the beliefs that give meaning to these social phenomena in order to achieve 'cultural unity'.[30]

Those sympathetic to the recommendations of the Runnymede report might well want to respond to this by claiming that the committed forms of religious education faith schools often provide typically fail to value and respect the lifestyles and sexual orientations that do not accord with the traditional teachings of their faith. Likewise, they might also want to claim that they fail to respect the right of their pupils to autonomy in respect of their faiths, lifestyles and sexual orientations. Clearly, no faith school should be allowed to advocate or condone the ill-treatment of those who differ in faith, lifestyle or sexual orientation from that which their own faith advocates. However, to ensure the full compliance of faith schools with such a reasonable demand, it is not necessary to expect or require them to discontinue seeking to nurture in their pupils the faith of their sponsoring group. This applies equally to such lifestyles and sexual orientations as they might also wish to nurture on the basis of being commended by their religion.

The Runnymede report claimed that for any faith school to propound such teachings would necessarily prevent their pupils from appreciating and valuing diversity in all its forms. In response to this claim, two things may be said. First, to suggest, as did the Runnymede report, that faith schools should teach their pupils to value and appreciate all faiths, lifestyles and sexual orientations equally sits very uneasily alongside the right of children to decide for themselves what to believe. Second, and more importantly, the report offers no legitimate reason why any schools, let alone faith schools, should be expected to teach their pupils to appreciate and value positively and equally *all* faiths, lifestyles and forms of sexual orientation. Are there not some, even some of them that may be perfectly legal, that schools may have legitimate reason to teach their pupils not to value positively? What about the lifestyles of dissolute alcoholics who betray and abandon loved ones and dependents, ruin their careers and health, and squander their talents, for the sake of indulging their craving for drink? What about the sexual orientations of philanderers and home-wreckers? What about religions that teach their adherents to despise and shun those not of their faith?

The moment that it is conceded that there are some religions, lifestyles and sexual orientations that schools may legitimately teach their pupils not to value positively, no principled reason seems to exist why faith schools may not also rightly be able to teach their pupils that there are some lifestyles and sexual orientations which, if acted upon, would violate the ordinances of their religion, and which are for that reason to be avoided by adherents of it.

The argument from children's rights

Doubtless, the authors of the Runnymede report would respond to the forgoing line of argument by claiming that any such forms of teaching by faith schools would violate the right of their pupils to decide what to believe in these matters for themselves. However, the suggestion that children should be thought of as possessing such a general right flies in the face of the very idea of schooling, as well as the notion that they are in need of instruction about what is good as well as true. It equally flies in the face of the acknowledged human right that parents have for their children to receive an education that accords with their wishes in relation to religion. This parental human right is recognised by both the Universal Declaration of Rights as well as by the European Convention of Human Rights. Article 27 of the former expressly ascribes to parents the 'right to choose the kind of education that shall be given to their children'.[31] Article 2 of the first protocol of the latter expressly states that: 'In the exercise of any functions which it assumes in relation to education and to teaching, the State shall respect the right of parents to ensure such education and teaching is in conformity with their own religious and philosophical convictions.'[32]

There is no inherent reason why receipt by children of such committed forms of religious education need necessarily be inimical to the development in them of autonomy. However, for children to acquire autonomy, they first need some form of identity to enable them to be able to make considered choices. Such an identity is something that they can only acquire in the first instance other than autonomously, that is, on a basis otherwise than by their deciding for themselves what to believe and value. There is no reason why the nurturance by schools in pupils of a specific form of religious identity should be considered to be any more prejudicial to their eventual attainment of autonomy than would be their receipt of a purely secular education or one that confined what was taught about religion to a neutral account of all the world's main religions.

Conclusion

This completes our examination of the considerations adduced by the Runnymede report in favour of the central recommendations it makes concerning how faith schools need to change so as to become maximally supportive of community cohesion. None was found at all convincing. As such, we found no adequate reason given by the report why faith schools should act upon any of the recommendations it made. Indeed, in the course of our examination of those considerations, several others were mentioned that suggest that inter-communal relations and community cohesion would be better served by faith schools continuing as they are at present.

In sum, not only are the various changes in faith schools for which the Runnymede report called without adequate justification; there exist sound reasons why these schools should not make them. They should resist such calls to make them, as should all who value education, diversity and community cohesion, as well as the spiritual well-being and autonomy of children and the adults they will eventually become.

Notes

Foreword

1   MacEoin, D., *Music, Chess and Other Sins: Segregation, Integration and Muslim Schools in Britain*, London: Civitas, February 2009, available online only at: http://www.civitas.org.uk/pdf/MusicChessAndOtherSins.pdf

2   Dennis, N., *The Uncertain Trumpet: A History of Church of England School Education to AD 2001*, London: Civitas, August 2001.

3   Dennis, *The Uncertain Trumpet*, p. 17.

4   Burn, J., Griffiths, B., Marks, J., Pilington, P., Thompson, P., *Faith in Education: The role of the churches in education: A response to the Dearing Report on church schools in the new millennium*, London: Civitas, September 2001.

5   Archbishops' Council Church Schools Review Group: *The Way Ahead: Church of England Schools in the New Millennium*, London: Church House, 2001. A draft version of the report had been published in December 2000 on which comments were invited.

6   Department for Education and Employment (DfEE), Schools: Building on Success (green paper), London: DfEE, 12 February 2001.

Introduction: The Case Against Faith Schools

1   Bell, D., 'What does it mean to be a citizen?', Speech delivered to the Hansard Society, 17 January 2005; http://education.guardian.co .uk/faithschools/story/0,,1392281,00.html

2   Bell, 'What does it mean to be a citizen?'.

3   Bell, 'What does it mean to be a citizen?'

4   'Muslim school slams inspector', *The Huddersfield Daily Examiner*, 18 January 2005.

5   Coughlan, S., 'Muslims schools "deeply upset"', *BBC News*, 18 January 2001.

6   Taylor, M., 'Two thirds oppose state aided faith schools', *Guardian*, 23 August 2006.

7   Taylor,' Two thirds oppose state aided faith schools'.

8   The Humanist Philosophers' Group, *Religious Schools: the case against*, London: British Humanist Association, 2001.

9   The Humanist Philosophers' Group, *Religious Schools*, p. 35.

10 The Humanist Philosophers' Group, *Religious Schools*, p. 10.

11 The Humanist Philosophers' Group, *Religious Schools*, p. 8.

161

2: Are Faith Schools Divisive?

1   Chowdhury, T., Mali, M, Halstead, J.M., Bunglawla, Z. and Spalek, B., *British Muslims and Education*, Budapest and New York: Open Society Institute, 2005, p. 126.

2   Henry, J., 'Half of Muslim schools not inspected', *Sunday Telegraph*, 4 March 2007.

3   McVeigh, T., 'Faith schools spark fear of "apartheid"', *Guardian*, 30 September 2001.

4   Taylor, M., 'Two thirds oppose state aided faith schools', *Guardian*, 23 August 2006.

3: Muslim Schools and Social Cohesion

1   For the view that Islam is inherently incompatible with the values of Western liberal democracy, see Ibn Warraq, *Why I Am Not a Muslim*, New York: Prometheus Books, 1995, esp. Ch.5. For a decisive refutation of that view, see Mohamed Charfi, *Islam and Liberty: The Historical Misunderstanding*, London and New York, 2005.

2   Goodman, P., 'Not Enough Islam? How mainstream Islam can challenge extremism', Talk delivered to The New Culture Forum, London, on 23 January 2008.

3   Quoted in Allen, C., *God's Terrorists: The Wahhabi Cult and the Hidden Roots of Modern Jihad*, first published 2006, London: Abacus, 2007, p. 207.

4   Allen, *God's Terrorists*, pp. 207-209 *passim*.

5   Kepel, G., *Allah in the West: Islamic Movements in America and Europe*, Stanford, California: Stanford University Press, 1997, p. 90.

6   Thornton, T., 'Deobandi Movement' in *History of the Middle East Database*; http://www.nmbschool.org/tthornton/deobandi_muslims.php.

7   Norfolk, A., 'A movement fostered by the fear of "imperial" rule', *The Times*, 7 September 2007.

8   Norfolk, 'A movement fostered by the fear of "imperial" rule'.

9   Morgan, A., 'The Talibanisation of Britain', *Family Security Matters*, 11 September 2007; http://www.westernresistance.com/blog/archives/003856.html.

10 ul-Haq, R., 'The Globalised Suffering of the Muslims', *The Times*, 6 September 2007.

11 Norfolk, A., 'The home-grown cleric who loathes the British', *The Times*, 7 September 2007.

12 ul-Haq, R., 'Imitating the Disbelievers', *The Times*, 6 September 2007.

13 ul-Haq, 'Imitating the Disbelievers'.

14 Norfolk, A., 'Hardline takeover of British mosques', *The Times*, 7 September 2007.

15 http://www.uclan.ac.uk/facs/class/edustud/staf/chandia.htm

16 Rangooni, H.E.Y.B, *The Importance of Islamic Education and Training*, Gloucester: Idara Isha'at al-Ilam, 1995, pp. 17-20 *passim*; quoted in Siskand, Y.B., 'The Origins and Growth of the *Tablighi Jamaat* in Britain', *Islam and Christian-Muslim Relations*, vol. 9, no. 2, 1998, pp. 171-92, pp.185-86.

17 Rangooni, H.E.Y.B, *Al Islam Bartanniya* vol. 2, 1996, pp. 25-26, quoted in Siskand, 'The Origins and Growth of the *Tablighi Jamaat* in Britain', p. 189.

18 Langley, W., 'Authorities Probe Little-Known Islamic Group's Alleged Ties to Extremists', *New York Sun*, 21 August 2006.

19 Gardham, D. and Rayner, G., 'Three British Muslims guilty of conspiracy to murder', *Telegraph*, 9 September 2008.

20 Sachs, S., 'A Muslim Missionary Group Draws New Scrutiny in U.S.', *New York Times*, 14 July 2003.

21 Ofsted, Report on Institute of Islamic Education, Inspection date: 28 February 2005; published: 17 October 2006; http://www.ofsted.gov.uk/reports/pdf/?inspectionNumber=109927&providerCategoryID=16384&fileName=\\school\\107\\s163_107791_20061017.pdf.

22 Ofsted, Report on Institute of Islamic Education, Inspection date: 20-21 May 2008; Published: 12 June 2008; http://www.ofsted.gov.uk/reports/pdf/?inspectionNumber=321812&providerCategoryID=16384&fileName=\\school\\107\\s163_107791_20080612.pdf

23 Greenhill, S. and Clark, L., 'Veil teacher link to 7/7 bomber', *Daily Mail*, 21 October 2006.

24 Norfolk, A., 'How bombers' town is turning into an enclave for Muslims', *The Times*, 21 October 2006.

25 Gilliat-Ray, S., 'Educating the *Ulama*: Centres of Islamic Religious Training in Britain', *Islam and Christian-Muslim Relations*, vol. 17, January 2006, pp. 55-76, p. 68.

26 Hussain, D., 'The need for home-grown imams', 2003, pp. 2-3, quoted in Gilliat-Ray, 'Educating the *Ulama*', p. 67.

27 Ofsted, 'Inspection Report: Jamiah Al'Hudaa: 5-6 February 2008', Unique ref.
    no: 134574.
    http://www.ofsted.gov.uk/reports/pdf/?inspectionNumber=320166&providerCa
    tegoryID=16384&fileName=\\school\\134\\s163_134574_20080222.pdf

28 'Palestine Loves Saddam', *Israel Behind the News*, 14 April 2003;
    http://israelbehindthenews.com/Archives/Apr-14-03.htm

29 Marcus, I and Crook, B., 'PA gets $50m from US, then calls for terror against US
    soldiers', *Palestinian Media Watch*, 6 September 2005; http://pmw.org.il/Hate-
    USA-Part4.htm

30 Gateway to Divine Mercy event, Manchester 2007;
    http://www.gatewaytodivinemercy.com/about.html;
    http://www.gatewaytodivinemercy.com/scholars.html

31 Pirzada, M.G., 'From al-Aqsa to al-Karam: UK Tour of Shaykh Yusuf Abu
    Sneina, Imam a& Khatib al-Aqsa, Jerusalem', *Official website of Shaykh Pirzada*, 4
    July 2006; http://www.mihpirzada.com/news/uktour2006.html

32 Frean, A., 'Teacher accuses Islamic school of racism', *The Times*, 15 April 2008.

33 Frean, 'Teacher accuses Islamic school of racism'.

34 Frean, 'Teacher accuses Islamic school of racism'.

35 MacEoin, D., *The Hijacking of British Islam: How extremist literature is subverting
    mosques in the UK*, London: Policy Exchange, 2007, p. 52.

36 MacEoin, *The Hijacking of British Islam*, p. 55.

37 MacEoin, *The Hijacking of British Islam*, p. 58.

38 Ofsted, 'Inspection Report: King Fahad Academy: 13-16 March 2006' DfES ref
    no: 307/6068.
    http://www.ofsted.gov.uk/reports/pdf/?inspectionNumber=285234&providerCa
    tegoryID=16384&fileName=\\school\\101\\s163_101957_20060407.pdf

39 Henry, J., 'Half of Muslim schools not inspected', *Sunday Telegraph*, 4 March
    2007.

40 Office for Standards in Education, *The Annual Report of Her Majesty's Chief
    Inspector of Schools 2003/4*, quoted in Meer, N., 'Muslim Schools in Britain:
    Challenging mobilisations or logical developments?', *Asia Pacific Journal of
    Education*, vol. 27, no. 1 March 2007, 55-71, p. 56.

41 'Who inspects schools?', *Telegraph News*, 31 January 2008;
    http://www.telegraph.co.uk/news/newstopics/politics/education/1577138/Who-
    inspects-schools.html

42 'Faith schools to get own vetting', *BBC News*, 31 January 2008.

43 Paton, G., 'Muslim schools to conduct own inspections', *Telegraph News*, 4 February 2008.

44 Wynne-Jones, J., 'Muslims want to opt-out of Ofsted inspections', *Telegraph News*, 10 September 2006.

45 Paton, 'Muslim schools to conduct own inspections'.

46 Ofsted Report on Leicester Islamic Academy, 29 April-3 May 2002, para. 67; http://www.ofsted.gov.uk/reports/pdf/?inspectionNumber=108661&providerCategoryID=16384&fileName=\\school\\120\\s163_120335_20061017.pdf

47 Ofsted Report on Leicester Islamic Academy 29 April-3 May 2002, para. 43.

48 Berliner, W., 'Wise and wonderful?', *Guardian*, 16 March 2004.

49 Helm, T., 'Holocaust Day must be scrapped, say Muslim leaders', *Telegraph News,,* 13 September 2005.

4: Faith Schools in General and Social Cohesion

1   The Education Reform Act 1988: Religious Education and Collective Worship, section 7.1.

2   The Education Reform Act 1988, section 8.3.

3   *Hansard*. HL., 21 June 1988, col. 717, quoted in Thompson, P., *Whatever Happened to Religious Education?*, Cambridge: The Lutterworth Press, 2004, p. 112.

4   *Hansard*, H.L., 21 June 1988, col. 718, quoted in Thompson, *Whatever Happened to Religious Education?*, p. 112.

5   DfES Circular 1/94.

6   'Letter to Mr [Fred] Naylor dated 25 March 1997 from C. Drury of the Curriculum and Assessment Division of the DfES (emphasis in the original). Section 375 (2) of the 1996 Act replaces Section 26 of the 1944 Act'. Thompson, *Whatever Happened to Religious Education?*, p. 185 endnote 53.

7   This section is very indebted to the line of argument developed by Penny Thompson in her book, *Whatever Happened to Religious Education?*

8   I owe this line of argument to Haldane, J., 'Religious Education in a Pluralist Society: A Philosophical Examination', *British Journal of Educational Studies*, vol. 34, no. 2, 1986, pp 161- 81.

9   Toynbee, P., 'Keep God out of class', *Guardian*, 9 November 2001.

10 Taylor, P., 'Two thirds oppose state aided faith schools', *Guardian*, 23 August 2005.

11 Office for National Statistics, 'Religious Populations: Christianity is main religion in Britain', National Statistics Online, 11 October 2004; http://www.statistics.gov.uk/cci/nugget.asp?id=954

12 Jones, S., '72 % have belief in a god', *Guardian*, 10 December 2004.

13 *BBC News*, 'Britons "back Christian society"' , 14 November 2005; http://news.bbc.co.uk/go/pr/fr/-/1/hi/uk/4434096.stm

14 Gledhill, R., 'God moves in a gender neutral way in latest prayer book', *The Times*, 19 May 2008.

15 Bauckham, I., 'Providing choice in good faith', *Secondary Headship*, June 2006; re-published by *Teaching expertise*; http://www.teachingexpertise.com/articles/providing-choice-in-good-faith-1021

5: Faith Schools as Agents of Cohesion

1 Hannam, L., 'Revealed: racism in schools', *Channel 4 News*, 24 May 2007; http://www.channel4.com/news/articles/society/education/revealed+racism+in+schools/529297.

2 Hannam, 'Revealed: racism in schools'.

3 Hannam, 'Revealed: racism in schools'.

4 Lipsett, A. 'UK schools worst in Europe for bullying', *Education Guardian*, 29 February 2008; http://education.guardian.co.uk/pupilbehaviour/story/0,,2261124,00.html

5 Osler, A., *Faith Schools and Community Cohesion: Observations on Community Consultations*, London: The Runnymede Trust, 2007.

6 Osler, *Faith Schools and Community Cohesion*, p. 7.

7 Osler, *Faith Schools and Community Cohesion*, p.10

8 Osler, *Faith Schools and Community Cohesion*, p.11.

9 Osler, *Faith Schools and Community Cohesion*, p. 12.

10 Osler, *Faith Schools and Community Cohesion*, p. 12.

11 Ansari, H., *'The Infidel Within': Muslims in Britain since 1800*, London: Hurst and Co., 2004, p. 308.

12 Office for National Statistics, *Focus on Religion*, London: Office for National Statistics, 2004, p. 12.

13 Chowdhury, T., Mali, M, Halstead, J.M., Bunglawla, Z. and Spalek, B., *British Muslims and Education*, Budapest and New York: Open Society Institute, 2005, p. 135.

14 Chowdhury, Malik, Halstead, Bunglawla, and Spalek, *British Muslims and Education*, pp. 135-36.

15 Chowdhury, Malik, Halstead, Bunglawla, and Spalek, *British Muslims and Education*. p. 138.

16 Short, G., 'Faith-Based Schools: A Threat to Social Cohesion?', *Journal of Philosophy of Education*, vol. 36, no. 4, 2002, 559-72, p. 565.

17 Cassen, R. and Kingdon, G., *Tackling Low Educational Achievement*, London: Joseph Rowntree Foundation, 2007. Findings.

18 Wilson, G., 'White, poor, male – and doomed to fail', *Telegraph*, 16 November, 2006.

19 Wilson, 'White, poor, male – and doomed to fail'.

20 Baring, K., 'Radical Insiders', *BBC TV Features* , 6 August 2007.

21 Malik, S., 'Are "Muslim Boys" using profits of crime to fund terrorist attacks?', *Independent*, 14 August 2005.

22 Phillips, T., 'After 7/7: Sleepwalking to Segregation', Speech delivered at the Manchester Council for Community Relations, 22 September 2005, Commission for Racial Equality Website.

23 *BBC News*, 'Black Boys separate classes idea', 7 March 2005.

24 Short, G., 'Faith Schools and Social Cohesion: Opening Up the Debate', *British Journal of Religious Education*, 2003, 25:2, 129-41.

25 Allport, G., *The Nature of Prejudice*, Cambridge, Mass: Addison-Wesley, 1954, p. 265, quoted in Short, 'Faith Schools and Social Cohesion', p. 132.

26 Short, 'Faith Schools and Social Cohesion', p. 138.

27 Short, 'Faith Schools and Social Cohesion', pp. 136-39 *passim*.

6: Faith Schools and Pupil Autonomy

1 Bradley, F.H., *Ethical Studies*, second edition 1927, Wollheim, R. (ed.), London: Oxford University Press, 1962, pp. 171-74 *passim*.

2 Lomasky, L.E., *Persons, Rights, and the Moral Community*, New York and Oxford: Oxford University Press, 1987, pp. 249-50.

3 Mitchell, B., 'Being Religiously Educated' in Leonard, G. and Yates, J. (eds), *Faith for the Future: Essays on the Church of England to mark 175 years of the National Society*, London: National Society Church House Publishing, 1986, 43-52, pp. 45-46.

4   Temple, W., Speech to the National Society , 1944, as quoted in Iremonger, F.A., *William Temple: Archbishop of Canterbury – His Life and Character*, London: Oxford University Press, 1948, p. 571.

5   Stephen, J.F., *Liberty, Equality, Fraternity*, first published 1873, Indianapolis: Liberty Fund, 1993, pp. 212-13.

6   MacMullen, I., *Faith in Schools?: Autonomy, Citizenship, and Religious Education in the Liberal State*, Princeton and Oxford: Princeton University Press, 2007, p. 186.

7   MacMullen, *Faith in Schools?*, pp. 188-89.

7: Faith Schools and Fairness

1   Pennell, H., West, A. and Hind, A., 'Religious Composition and Admission Processes of Faith Secondary Schools in London', Education Research Group, Department of Social Policy, London School of Economics, May 2007, p.3. http://www.lse.ac.uk/collections/ERG/pdf/FaithSchoolsMay2007%5B1%5D.pdf

2   Pennell, West and Hind, 'Religious Composition and Admission Processes of Faith Secondary Schools in London', p. 11.

3   Tough, S. and Brooks, R., *School Admissions: Fair choice for parents and pupils*, London: Institute for Public Policy Research, 2007, p. 16.

4   Tough and Brooks, *School Admissions*, p. 16.

5   Tough and Brooks, *School Admissions*, p. 19.

6   Gledhill, R., 'Backlash as more claim religion to get place in top schools', *The Times*, 12 January 2008.

7   Gledhill, 'Backlash as more claim religion to get place in top schools'.

8   Petre, J., 'Children baptised to get into Catholic schools', *Daily Telegraph*, 13 January 2008.

9   Smith, J. Speech in Debate on Admissions Policies of Faith Schools, Westminster Hall, 14 February 2006; column 389WH http://www.publications.parliament.uk/pa/cm200506/cmhansrd/vo060214/hallte xt/60214h01.htm#column_367

10 Smith, Speech in Debate on Admissions Policies of Faith Schools.

11 Bauckham, I., 'Providing choice in good faith', *Secondary Headship*, June 2006; re-published by *Teaching expertise*; http://www.teachingexpertise.com/articles/providing-choice-in-good-faith-1021

12 Holness, M., 'Church schools not "cherry-picking" say C of E officers', *Church Times*, 21 September 2007.

13 Butt, R., 'The best of both worlds', *Guardian News*, 13 May 2008.

14 Butt, The best of both worlds'.

15 Woolcock, N., 'Privileged children excel, even at low-performing comprehensives', *The Times*, 21 February 2008.

9: The Governments Community Cohesion Agenda—The Making of a Legend

1 Ouseley, H., *Community Pride not Prejudice: Making diversity work in Bradford*, Bradford: Bradford Vision, 2001, Preface.

2 Ouseley, *Community Pride Not Prejudice*, 1.1 [All reference to numbered paragraphs]

3 Ritchie, D., *Oldham Independent Review: One Oldham One Future*, Manchester: Government Office for the North West, 2001, 1.11.

4 Ritchie, *Oldham Independent Review*, 3.8.

5 Ritchie, *Oldham Independent Review*, 1.15.

6 Ritchie, *Oldham Independent Review*, 2.7.

7 Ritchie, *Oldham Independent Review*, 2.7.

8 Clarke, T., *Burnley Speaks, Who Listens?*, Burnley: Burnley Borough Council, 2001, p. 33.

9 Clarke, *Burnley Speaks*, p. 48.

10 Clarke, *Burnley Speaks*, p. 55

11 Cantle, T., *Community Cohesion: A report of the independent review team*, London: Home Office, 2001, 2.1 and 2.3. [All references to numbered paragraphs.]

12 Denham, J., *Building Cohesive Community: A report of the ministerial group on public order and community cohesion*, London: Home Office, 2001, Introduction, 7. [All references to numbered paragraphs.]

13 Simpson, L., 'Statistics of Racial Segregation: Measures, Evidence and Policy', *Urban Studies*, vol. 4, no. 3, March 2004, pp. 661-681, pp., 668-69.

14 Simpson, 'Statistics of Racial Segregation', p. 674.

15 Simpson, 'Statistics of Racial Segregation', p. 677.

16 Cantle, *Community Cohesion*, 5.10.7.

17 Cantle, *Community Cohesion*, 5.10.8.

18 McRoy, A., *From Rushdie to 7/7: The Radicalisation of Islam in Britain*, London: Social Affairs Unit, 2006, pp. 28-37.

19 McRoy, From Rushdie to 7/7, p. 30.

20 McRoy, From Rushdie to 7/7, p. 30.

21 McRoy, From Rushdie to 7/7, p. 30.

22 McRoy, From Rushdie to 7/7, p. 31.

23 McRoy, From Rushdie to 7/7, p. 32.

24 McRoy, From Rushdie to 7/7, p. 37.

10: The Contact Hypothesis Examined

1   Allport, G.W., *The Nature of Prejudice*, Reading, Mass.: Addison-Wesley, 1954.

2   Home Office, *Building a Picture of Community Cohesion: A guide for Local Authorities and their partners*, London: Home Office Community Cohesion Unit, 2003), p. 5.

3   *Statistical Release of Citizenship Survey: April-June 2007, England and Wales*, London: Department for Communities and Local Government, 2008, p. 6.

4   Hudson, M., Phillips, J., Ray K. and Barnes, H., 'Social cohesion in diverse communities', York: Joseph Rowntree Foundation, 2007, p. 30.

5   Vertovec, S., 'New Complexities of Cohesion in Britain: Super-diversity, transnationalism and civil-integration', Oxford: COMPAS, 2007, p. 3.

6   Vertovec, 'New Complexities of Cohesion in Britain', p. 6.

7   Vertovec, 'New Complexities of Cohesion in Britain', pp. 34-40 *passim*.

8   Vertovec, 'New Complexities of Cohesion in Britain', p. 40. I have transposed some sentences in this quotation.

9   Smith, A., *The Theory of Moral Sentiments*, Sixth Edition 1790, Indianapolis, Indiana: Liberty Fund, 1982, pp. 223-24.

10 Commission on Integration and Cohesion, *Our Shared Futures*, London: Department of Communities and Local Government, 2007, paragraph 8.3.

11 Putnam, R.D., *Bowling Alone*, New York: Simon and Schuster, 2000.

12 Putnam, *Bowling Alone*, p. 362.

13 Gordon, M. M., *Assimilation in American Life*, New York: Oxford University Press, 1964, pp. 164-65.

14 Forbes, H.D., *Ethnic Conflict: Commerce, Culture and the Contact Hypothesis*, New Haven and London: Yale University Press, 1997.

15 Forbes, *Ethnic Conflict*, pp. 58-60 *passim*. Some quoted sentences have been transposed for easier reading.

16 Harris, D., Hendry, K. and Kongshaug, N., 'Lessons of Little Rock: Fifty Years after desegregation, Central High School remains divided', *ABC News*, 23 September 2007.

17 Neuman, E., 'Finding freedom in self-segregation—African Americans' preference for black suburbs' , *Insight on the News*, 6 June 1994; http://findarticles.com/p/articles/mi_m1571/is_n23_v10/ai_15461434/pg_1

18 Neuman, 'Finding freedom in self-segregation'.

19 Schlesinger, A.M., *The Disuniting of America: Reflections on a multicultural society*, first published 1991, New York and London: Norton, 1993, pp. 103-07.

20 Bennett, W.J., *The De-Valuing of America: The Fight for Our Culture and Our Children*, New York: Touchstone, 1992, pp. 183-86.

21 Bork, R.H., *Slouching Towards Gomorrah: Modern liberalism and American decline*, first published 1996, New York: Harper Collins, 1997, p. 300.

22 Bork, Slouching Towards Gomorrah, pp. 300-305 *passim*.

23 Highfield, R., 'Harvard's baby brain research lab', *Daily Telegraph*, 30 April 2008; http://www.telegraph.co.uk/earth/main.jhtml?view=DETAILS&grid=&xml=/earth/2008/04/30/sm_babies03.xml

24 Rogers, B. and Muir, R., *The Power of Belonging: Identity, citizenship and community cohesion*, London: Institute for Public Policy Research, 2007, p. 6.

25 Rogers and Muir, *The Power of Belonging*, p. 6.

26 Muir, R., *One London?: Change and cohesion in three London boroughs* London: Institute for Public Policy Research, 2008, p. 15.

27 Laurence, J. and Heath, A., *Predictors of Community Cohesion: Multi-level modelling of the 2005 Citizenship Survey*, London: Department for Communities and Local Government, 2008, p. 44.

28 Laurence and Heath, *Predictors of Community Cohesion*, p. 44.

29 CIC, *Our Shared Futures*, paragraph 2.6.

11: School Twinning

1 DfES Press Release, 'Johnson Says Pupils Need to Learn Our History to Understand British Values in Citizenship Classes', 25 January 2007.

2 DfES Press Release, 'Johnson Says Pupils Need to Learn Our History to Understand British Values in Citizenship Classes'.

3 DCSF, *Guidance on the duty to promote community cohesion*, 2007, p. 9.

4 DCSF, *Guidance on the duty to promote community cohesion*, 2007, p. 9.

5 Homepage of the Schools Linking Network;
http://www.schoolslinkingnetwork.org.uk

6 Land, J., 'School pupils encouraged to celebrate diversity and build "community cohesion"', 24dash.com, 23 June 2008; http://www.24dash.com.

7 Bruegel, I., 'Social Capital, Diversity and Education Policy', Families and Social Capital ESRC Research Group, London South Bank University, August 2006; http://www.lsbu.ac.uk/families/publications/SCDiversityEDu28.8.06.pdf

8 Raw, A., 'Schools Linking Project 2005-06: Full Final Evaluation Report', Bradford Schools Linking Evaluation Report;
http://www.bradfordschools.net/slp/content/view/70/153/#slnr

9 Bruegel, 'Social Capital, Diversity and Education Policy', p. 6.

10 Bruegel, 'Social Capital, Diversity and Education Policy', p. 6.

11 Raw, 'Schools Linking Project 2005-06: Full Final Evaluation Report', p. 9.

12 Raw, 'Schools Linking Project 2005-06: Full Final Evaluation Report', p. 11.

13 Raw, 'Schools Linking Project 2005-06: Full Final Evaluation Report', p. 11.

14 Raw, 'Schools Linking Project 2005-06: Full Final Evaluation Report', p. 59.

15 Bruegel, 'Social Capital, Diversity and Education Policy', p. 9.

12: Forced Contact Between Communities

1 Forbes, H.D., *Ethnic Conflict: Commerce, Culture and the Contact Hypothesis*, New Haven and London: Yale University Press, 1997,
pp. 146-48 *passim*.

2 Putnam, R.D., *Bowling Alone*, New York: Simon and Schuster, 2000, p. 19.

3 Putnam, R.D., '*E Pluribus Unum*: Diversity and community in the twenty-first century', *Scandinavian Political Studies* 30 (2) 2007, 137-74. Page references to web version: http://www.www.blackwell-synergy.com/doi/fabs.10.1111/j.1467-9477.2007.00176.x

4 Putnam, '*E Pluribus Unum*', p. 8.

5 Putnam, '*E Pluribus Unum*', pp. 10-11.

6 'Bowling with Robert Putnam', *The American Interest*, vol. III, no. 3, Jan/Feb 2008, p. 5.

7 'Bowling with Robert Putnam', p.13.

8   'Bowling with Robert Putnam', pp. 17-18.

13: Interculturalism—Meet the New Boss

1   Kiwan, D., 'A Journey to Citizenship in the United Kingdom', *International Journal on Multicultural Societies*, vol. 10, no. 1, 2008, pp. 60-75, p. 66.

2   Kiwan, D., 'Memorandum' (7 June 2006) in House of Commons Education and Skills Committee, *Citizenship Education*, Second Report of Session 2006-07, London: House of Commons, 2007, Ev. 125.23.

3   Kiwan, 'Memorandum', Ev. 125.24.

4   Clark, D., 'Memorandum', 24 October 2005, in *Citizenship Education*, Ev. 11.

5   Commission for Racial Equality, 'Memorandum', 7 June 2006, in *Citizenship Education*, Ev. 105

6   Development Education Association, 'Memorandum', March 2006, in *Citizenship Education*, Ev. 234.

7   Starkey, H., 'Memorandum', March 2006, in *Citizenship Education*, Ev. 239.

8   Regent College, 'Memorandum', March 2006, in *Citizenship Education*, Ev. Ev.252.

9   Nesbitt, E., *Intercultural Education: Ethnographic and religious approaches*, Brighton and Portland, Oregon: Sussex Academic Press, 2004, p. 163.

10 Vickery, W.E. and Cole, S.G., *Intercultural Education in American Schools: Proposed objectives and methods*, New York and London: Harper and Brothers, 1943, p. xv.

11 Vickery and Cole, *Intercultural Education in American Schools*, p. 176.

12 Vickery and Cole, *Intercultural Education in American Schools*, p. 155.

13 Vickery and Cole, *Intercultural Education in American Schools*, p. 167.

14 Vickery and Cole, *Intercultural Education in American Schools*, p. 167.

15 Batelaan, P., *The Practice of Intercultural Education*, London: Commission for Racial Equality, 1983, pp. 16-17.

16 Gundara, J.S., *Interculturalism, Education and Inclusion*, London: Sage, 2000.

17 Gundara, *Interculturalism, Education and Inclusion*, pp. 24-25.

18 Gundara, *Interculturalism, Education and Inclusion*, p.28.

19 Gundara, *Interculturalism, Education and Inclusion*, p. 70.

20 Gundara, *Interculturalism, Education and Inclusion*, p. 71.

21 Gundara, *Interculturalism, Education and Inclusion*, p. 71.

22 Gundara, *Interculturalism, Education and Inclusion*, p. 57.

23 Gundara, *Interculturalism, Education and Inclusion*, p. 72.

24 Gundara, *Interculturalism, Education and Inclusion*, p. 76.

25 Gundara, *Interculturalism, Education and Inclusion*, p. 123.

26 Gundara, J., *Intercultural Education: World on the brink?*, London: Institute of Education, University of London, 2003, p. 8.

27 Gundara, *Intercultural Education*, p. 10.

28 Ouseley, H., *Community Pride not Prejudice: Making diversity work in Bradford*, Bradford: Bradford Vision, 2001, 3.4.

29 Ouseley, *Community Pride Not Prejudice*, 4.13.10.

30 Ouseley, *Community Pride Not Prejudice*, 6.

31 Ritchie, D., *Oldham Independent Review: One Oldham One Future*, Manchester: Government Office for the North West, 2001, 2.5.

32 Ritchie, *Oldham Independent Review*, 2.6.

33 Clarke, T., *Burnley Speaks, Who Listens?*, Burnley: Burnley Borough Council, 2001, 3.4.

34 Cantle, T., *Community Cohesion: A report of the independent review team*, London: Home Office, 2001, 4.8.

35 Cantle, *Community Cohesion*, 4.8.

36 Cantle, *Community Cohesion*, 5.1.4.

37 Cantle, *Community Cohesion*, 5.1.7.

38 Cantle, *Community Cohesion*, 5.1.15.

39 Cantle, *Community Cohesion*, 5.8.13.

40 Cantle, *Community Cohesion*, 6.36.

41 Cantle, *Community Cohesion*, 6.36.

42 Cantle, *Community Cohesion*, 6.37.

43 Cantle, *Community Cohesion*, 6.38.

44 Denham, J., *Building Cohesive Community: A report of the ministerial group on public order and community cohesion*, London: Home Office, 2001, 3.12.

45 Home Office, *Improving Opportunity and Strengthening Society: The Government's strategy to increase race equality and community cohesion*, London: Home Office, 2005, pp. 42-43.

46 Home Office, *Improving Opportunity and Strengthening Society*, p. 42.

47 Home Office, *Improving Opportunity and Strengthening Society*, p. 46.

48 Home Office, *Improving Opportunity and Strengthening Society*, p. 44.

49 Ajegbo. K, *Diversity and Citizenship: Curriculum review*, Nottingham: Department for Education and Skills, 2007, p. 12.

50 Ajegbo, *Diversity and Citizenship*, p. 15.

51 Ajegbo, *Diversity and Citizenship*, p. 98.

52 Ajegbo, *Diversity and Citizenship*, pp. 98-99.

53 Commission on Integration and Cohesion, *Our Shared Futures*, London: Department of Communities and Local Government, 2007, paragraph, 4.8.

54 CIC, *Our Shared Futures*, 8.10.

55 CIC, *Our Shared Futures*, 8.10

56 CIC, *Our Shared Futures*, 8.11.

57 CIC, *Our Shared Futures*, 8.12.

58 CIC, *Our Shared Futures*, 8.18.

59 CIC, *Our Shared Futures*, 8.19.

60 Department for Children, Schools and Families (DCSF), *Guidance on the Duty to Promote Community Cohesion*, July 2007, p. 1.

61 DCFS, *Guidance on the Duty to Promote Community Cohesion*, p. 7.

62 DCFS, *Guidance on the Duty to Promote Community Cohesion*, p. 7.

63 Department of Communities and Local Government, *The Government's Response to the Commission on Integration and Cohesion*, London: Department of Communities and Local Government, 2008, para. 3.19.

14: A Closer Look At the Ajegbo Report

1 Ajegbo. K, *Diversity and Citizenship: Curriculum review*, Nottingham: Department for Education and Skills, 2007, p. 60.

2 Ajegbo, *Diversity and Citizenship*, p. 63.

3 Ajegbo, *Diversity and Citizenship*, p. 12.

4 Ajegbo, *Diversity and Citizenship*, p. 16.

5 See Conway, D., *A Nation of Immigrants?: A brief demographic history of Britain*, London: Civitas, 2007.

6   Trevelyan, G.M., *Illustrated History of England*, first published 1926, third edition, London, New York and Toronto, 1956, p. 1.

7   Bryant, A., *The Story of England: Makers of the realm*, London: Collins, 1961, p. 19.

8   Rowse, A.L., *The Spirit of English History*, London: Jonathan Cape, 1943, p. 10.

9   Rowse, *The Spirit of English History*, p. 30.

10 Rowse, *The Spirit of English History*, pp. 78-79.

11 Ajegbo, *Diversity and Citizenship*, p. 100.

12 Ajegbo, *Diversity and Citizenship*, p. 101.

13 Ajegbo, *Diversity and Citizenship*, p. 101.

14 Ajegbo, *Diversity and Citizenship*, p. 103.

15 Ajegbo, *Diversity and Citizenship*, p. 103.

16 Ajegbo, *Diversity and Citizenship*, p. 105.

17 Ajegbo, *Diversity and Citizenship*, p. 106.

18 Ajegbo, *Diversity and Citizenship*, p. 107.

19 Ajegbo, *Diversity and Citizenship*, pp. 107-08.

20 Ajegbo, Diversity and Citizenship, p.6.

21 Hewitt, R., *White Backlash and the Politics of Multiculturalism*, Cambridge: Cambridge University Press, 2005, p. 123.

22 Hewitt, *White Backlash*, p. 126.

23 McGovern, C., 'The New History Boys' in Whelan, R., (ed.) *The Corruption of the Curriculum*, London: Civitas, 2007, pp. 68-69.

24 McGovern, 'The New History Boys', pp. 74-75.

15: Interculturalism Refuted

1   Schwartz, B., 'The Diversity Myth', *The Atlantic Monthly*, May 1995; http://www.theatlantic.com/politics/foreign/divers.htm

2   Gordon, M.M., *Assimilation in American Life: The role of race, religion, and national origins*, New York: Oxford University Press, 1964, pp. 194-95.

3   Gordon, *Assimilation in American Life*, pp. 129-30.

4   Huntington, S.P., *Who Are We? America's great debate*, London: Sion and Schuster, 2004, p. 183.

16: A Better Pathway to Cohesion

1   Fonte, J., 'We Need a Patriotic Assimilation Policy', *American Outlook*, Winter 2003 issue; Hudson Institute, 14 May 2003.

2   Fonte, 'We Need a Patriotic Assimilation Policy'.

3   Fonte, 'We Need a Patriotic Assimilation Policy'.

4   Fonte, 'We Need a Patriotic Assimilation Policy'.

5   Lord Goldsmith, *Citizenship: Our common bond*, London: Ministry of Justice, 2008; http://www.justice.gov.uk/docs/citizenship-report-full.pdf

6   See Conway, D., 'Why History Remains the Best Form of Citizenship Education', *Civitas Review* vol 2, Issue 2, July 2005; http://www.civitas.org.uk/pdf/CivitasReviewJuly05.pdf

7   House of Commons Education and Skills Committee, *Citizenship Education*, p. 14. para. 33.

8   House of Commons Education and Skills Committee, *Citizenship Education*, p. 14. para. 34.

17: Conclusion: At the Going Down of the Sun

1   Ferguson, N., *Empire: How Britain made the modern world*, first published 2003, London and New York: Penguin Books, 2004, pp. 305-348 *passim*.

2   Tully, M., 'For your tomorrow we gave our today', *BBC News website*, 25 May 2007.

3   Review of Vidya Arnand, 'Indian Heroes and Heroines of World War ll', *Indian Journal*; republished *Rediff Homepages*; http://members.rediff.com/noorkhan/begum.htm

4   West Indian Ex Servicemen's Association, 'Latest VC Winner to Remember West Indian War Heroes', 16 May 2008; http://www.prnewswire.co.uk/cgi/news/release?id=170962

5   '24th May- Empire Day ... for Queen and Country!', *Historic –UK.com*; http://www.historic-uk.com/HistoryUK/England-History/EmpireDay.htm

6   '24th May- Empire Day ... for Queen and Country!'

7   Ferguson, N., *Empire*, pp. 338-63 *passim*.

8   Jenkins, L., *Disappearing Britain: The EU and the death of local government*, Washington DC: Orange State Press, 2005, pp. 169-70.

9   Jenkins, *Disappearing Britain*, p. 168.

10 Jenkins, *Disappearing Britain*, p. 168.

11 McDougall, W., *Ethics and Some Modern World Problems*, London: Methuen, 1924, pp. 46-47.

12 McDougall, *Ethics and Some Modern World Problems*, pp. 54-55 *passim*.

13 Body, R., *England for the English*, London: New European Publications, 2001, p. 2.

14 Body, *England for the English*, p. 2.

15 Body, *England for the English*, p. 5.

16 Body, *England for the English*, p. 8.

17 Body, *England for the English*, p. 5.

18 Body, *England for the English*, p. 6.

19 Body, *England for the English*, p.94.

20 Body, *England for the English*, p. 7.

21 Body, *England for the English*, p. 9.

22 Dunford, J.E., *Her Majesty's Inspectorate of Schools Since 1944: Standard bearers or turbulent priests?*, London and Portland, Oregon: Woburn Press, 1998, pp. 208-11 *passim*.

23 Macaulay, T.B., 'Speech to the House of Commons on the 10th of July 1833' in Macaulay, T.B., *Miscellaneous Writings and Speeches*, first published 1876, Popular Edition, London: Longmans, Green and Co., 1889, pp. 551-72; pp. 566-72 *passim*.

Appendix: A Response to the Runnymede Trust Report

1 Berkeley, R., *Right to Divide? Faith Schools and Community Cohesion*, London: Runnymede Trust, 2008.

2 Berkeley, *Right to Divide?*, p. 68.

3 Berkeley, *Right to Divide?*, p. 28.

4 Qualifications and Curriculum Authority, *The Non-Statutory National Framework for Religious Education*, London: Qualifications and Curriculum Authority, 2004; http://www.qca.org.uk/libraryAssets/media/9817_re_national_framework_04.pdf

5 Berkeley, *Right to Divide?*, p. 68.

6 See 'The Equality Act (Sexual Orientation) Regulations 2007, Guidance for Schools'; http://www.teachernet.gov.uk/docbank/index.cfm?id=12504

7   Berkeley, *Right to Divide?*, p. 39.

8   Berkeley, *Right to Divide?*, p. 29.

9   Berkeley, *Right to Divide?*, p. 68.

10 Berkeley, *Right to Divide?*, pp. 30-31.

11 Berkeley, *Right to Divide?*, p. 30.

12 Berkeley, *Right to Divide?*, p. 30.

13 Hogg, Q., *The Case for Conservatism* (Harmondsworth: Penguin, 1947), p. 23.

14 Greer, J., 'Viewing "the other side" in Northern Ireland', in Francis, L. and Lankshear, D. (eds), *Christian Perspectives on Church Schools*, Leominster: Gracewing Books, 1993), p. 456.

15 Short, G., 'Faith Schools and Social Cohesion: Opening Up the Debate', *British Journal of Religious Education*, 25:2, 129-41, p. 138.

16 Berkeley, *Right to Divide?*, p. 1.

17 See, for example, the contributions by Julia Ipgrave and by Robert Jackson to Jackson, R. (ed.), *International Perspectives on Ciitzenship, Education and Religious Diversity*, London: RoutledgeFalmer, 2003.

18 Lipsett, A., 'UK schools worst in Europe for bullying', *Education Guardian*, 29 February 2008.

19 Lipsett, 'UK schools worst in Europe for bullying'.

20 Berkeley, *Right to Divide?*, p. 68.

21 Swaine, J., 'Faith school pupils "outperforming others at every age"', *Telegraph*, 20 December 2008.

22 Swaine, 'Faith school pupils "outperforming others at every age"'.

23 Office for National Statistics, 'Religious Populations: Christianity is main religion in Britain', National Statistics Online, 11 October 2004; http://www.statistics.gov.uk/cci/nugget.asp?id=954.

24 Haldane, J., 'Religious Education in a Pluralist Society: A Philosophical Examination', *British Journal of Educational Studies*, vol. 34, no 2, 1985, 161-81, p. 176.

25 Office for National Statistics, 'Religious Populations: Christianity is main religion in Britain'.

26 See MacMullen, L., *Faith in Schools?: Autonomy, Citizenship and Religious Education in the Liberal State*, Princeton and London: Princeton University Press, 2007.

27 Hargreaves, D., *The Mosaic of Learning: Schools and Teachers for the Next Century*, London: Demos, 1994, p. 34.

28 Pearce, S., 'Swann and the Spirit of the Age', in Palmer, F. (ed.), *Anti-Education – An Assault on Education And Value*, London: Sherwood Press, 1986, pp. 136-48, p. 144.

29 Quoted in Gledhill, R., 'Archbishop sees apathy in secular school pupils', *The Times*, 12 September 2003.

30 Haldane, 'Religious Education in a Pluralist Society', p.165.

31 General Assembly of the United Nations, 'Universal Declaration of Human Rights', adopted 1948, Appendix IV of Melden, A.I. (ed.), *Human Rights*, Belmont, California: Wadsworth, 1970, p. 148.

32 Council of Europe, *The European Convention on Human Rights and its Five Protocols*, Rome 1950 and Paris 1952; http://www.hri.org/docs/ECHR50.html